WALK BY
Faith
NOT BY
Sexuality

WALK BY *Faith* NOT BY *Sexuality*

A COMPASSIONATE GUIDE *to* SEXUAL IDENTITY, RELIGIOUS INTEGRITY, *and* INNER PEACE

TERRY REESE *and* **SCOTT BEYER**

FOREWORD *by* RICH WYLER

terry@biblicalsexualintegrity.org

ISBN: 979-8-9903524-2-1 (paperback)
ISBN: 979-8-9903524-3-8 (ebook)
ISBN: 979-8-9903524-4-5 (hardcover)
ISBN: 979-8-9903524-5-2 (audiobook)

Library of Congress Control Number: 2024918447

Ordering Information:
Special discounts are available on quantity purchases by corporations, associations, and others. For details, contact terry@biblicalsexualintegrity.org

Unless otherwise indicated, all Scripture quotations are taken from the (NASB®) New American Standard Bible®, Copyright © 1960, 1971, 1977, 1995, 2020 by The Lockman Foundation. Used by permission. All rights reserved. lockman.org.

Scripture quotations marked (NLT) are taken from the Holy Bible, New Living Translation, copyright ©1996, 2004, 2015 by Tyndale House Foundation. Used by permission of Tyndale House Publishers, a Division of Tyndale House Ministries, Carol Stream, Illinois 60188. All rights reserved.

Publisher's Cataloging-in-Publication Data
Names: Reese, Terry, author. | Beyer, Scott, author.
Title: Walk by faith, not by sexuality : a compassionate guide to sexual identity, religious integrity, and inner peace / Terry Reese and Scott Beyer.

Note To The Reader

WE VALUE SELF-DISCOVERY HELPING INDIVIDUALS PROCESS SAME-SEX attractions in affirming ways that align with a person's faith, values, and life goals. We recognize the right of all people who experience same-sex attractions to choose their own sexual identity and how (or whether) to express it. We understand that for very personal reasons—and of their own volition—many members of faith communities seek to align their sexual thoughts, feelings, and behaviors with their personal values, beliefs, faith, commitments, and life goals as much as possible rather than the other way around.

In 2009, an American Psychological Association (APA) task force on appropriate therapeutic responses to sexual orientation recognized that not all individuals are suitable candidates for gay affirmative therapy (GAT) as traditionally practiced. Some individuals have personal or religious beliefs that make them unwilling or unable to engage in GAT if they already hold a predetermined opinion on resolving conflicts between faith and sexuality. The APA acknowledges that, for these individuals, alternative therapeutic models may be more appropriate. These models are client centered and identity focused, emphasizing social support and healthy coping mechanisms while allowing exploration of conflicts between sexual and religious identities.

Mark A. Yarhouse, Psy.D., author of *Sexual Identity & Faith: Helping Clients Find Congruence*, developed a Sexual Identity

Therapy protocol to guide clients in exploring their sexual identity through various Christian perspectives. Before the introduction of Sexual Identity Therapy, two contrasting approaches were prevalent: sexual orientation change efforts (SOCE) and gay affirmative therapy (GAT). Professional organizations have distanced themselves from SOCE, criticizing its aim of shifting clients toward a heterosexual orientation. This goal is widely discouraged due to doubts about its effectiveness and the understanding that homosexuality is not a mental illness, as recognized by major mental health organizations like the APA and the American Psychiatric Association.

In contrast, GAT focuses on integrating same-sex sexuality into both private and public identity, along with corresponding intimate relationships. While not a specific therapy protocol, GAT serves as a framework for individuals to navigate being gay, often leading to tensions with traditional religious beliefs. Recognizing the need for a safe environment to explore these tensions, Dr. Yarhouse developed Sexual Identity Therapy. This approach is client centered and identity focused, emphasizing healthy coping and social support without prescribing a predetermined outcome for the client's sexual identity or defining what achieving congruence means in the context of the client's beliefs and values.

In collaboration with Scott Beyer, we created Faith-Based Acceptance, Abstinence, Congruency, & Practice Therapy (FB-AACP), a subset of Christian viewpoints within Sexual Identity Therapy. This approach aligns with those who believe that orientation change may not (and need not) be expected, but who still have moral concerns about same-gender attractions and practices.

Individuals following FB-AACP Therapy typically refrain from using identity labels like "gay" or "queer" and may disidentify with aspects of the mainstream LGBTQ+ community. This perspective also aligns with the Christian thought found in Christopher Yuan's book *Holy Sexuality and the Gospel.*

For those interested in a review of various Christian viewpoints on the permissibility of same-sex relationships, Dr. Yarhouse's *Sexual Identity & Faith: Helping Clients Find Congruence* is highly recommended. This book (Walk by Faith, Not by Sexuality) is written from the perspective of a conservative Christian striving to live faithfully while experiencing conflicts with same-sex attractions, and ultimately finding peace within this journey.

Sincerely,

Terry Reese and Scott Beyer

Legal Disclaimer

The information provided in this book, including worksheets, therapeutic protocols, and informed consent forms, is designed for educational purposes and to support the work of qualified Christian or pastoral counselors. While the materials may be used by individuals or in a group settivng with the guidance of a pastor or support group leader, they are not intended to replace professional counseling, psychotherapy, or medical advice.

The application of these resources for self-help should be approached with caution. Readers are encouraged to seek personalized counseling or consult a qualified professional if they have specific mental health concerns or complex issues. Neither the author nor the publisher assumes responsibility for outcomes based on the use of the information or exercises in this book outside a professional therapeutic setting.

The Faith-Based, Acceptance, Abstinence, Congruency, and Practice (FAACP) protocol is intended to guide Christian spiritual growth and should be supplemented by the appropriate support of a trained professional or pastoral leader. It is not a substitute for evidence-based therapeutic practices.

Copyright Notice

All worksheets, forms, and protocols included in this book are protected by copyright. Unauthorized reproduction or distribution without the express permission of the author is prohibited. The materials may be used for personal development, small group study, or pastoral guidance, provided they are not altered or reproduced for commercial purposes.

‒ ‒ ‒ ‒ ‒ ‒ ‒ ‒ ‒ ‒ ‒ ‒ ‒ ‒ ‒ ‒ ‒ ‒ ‒ ‒

Foreword

TERRY REESE IS A MAN OF COURAGE.

Over the past 20-plus years, I've spoken with, mentored, coached, or otherwise worked with thousands of men who were conflicted over their same-sex attractions—men who found those attractions to be incongruent with their faith, beliefs, values, identity, and life goals. Very few of these men have had the courage to share their journey publicly for the benefit and hope of others.

Terry is one of the courageous few who has.

I first witnessed Terry's courage and openness in 2022 when he took the risk to participate in a weekend-long, deeply intensive workshop for men who are working through aspects of their incongruent same-sex attractions. I had pioneered the program called "Journey into Manhood" 20 years earlier and have since seen thousands of men ages 21 to 78 participate in order to vulnerably explore and heal their inner world. It is all too rare to see professional counselors who have the humility, curiosity, and courage to attend as just another participant rather than to insist on presenting themselves as a mental health expert who is above the need to do any healing work himself. But Terry immersed himself in the work. And his life has changed because of it.

Having walked this challenging journey himself, he now openly follows the same direction the Lord gave to Peter: "When you have repented and turned to me again, strengthen your brothers" (Luke 22:32 NLT). Or, as this idea is phrased in the Twelfth Step of the addiction-recovery programs, "Having had a spiritual awakening… we tried to carry this message to others…"

But Terry gives the reader much more than the benefit of his rich personal experience, as powerful as that is. He also shares his deep Christian faith and personal, healing relationship with Jesus Christ. Third, he brings decades of clinical experience as a trained and licensed professional counselor. This powerful combination of experience reminds me of Ecclesiastes 4:12: "A cord of three strands is not quickly broken" (NLT).

And knowing the power of witnesses (2 Corinthians 13:1), Terry has invited his close friend Scott Beyer, a dedicated preacher of the gospel of Christ, to join him in this work by providing wise and insightful biblical commentaries that affirm the truths of the principles shared here. Scott's perspective is especially poignant in that Scott has personally walked alongside Terry since 2006, supporting him through the messiness and beauty of struggle and redemption. Scott's contributions to this book are invaluable. In fact, their collaboration has culminated in the creation of a faith-based framework and clinical protocol that helps men respond to same-sex attractions in a biblically faithful way.

When Terry asked me to support and advise him as he and Scott developed *Walk by Faith Not by Sexuality*, I was honored, of course. However, I was particularly struck by the four key biblical principles on which he has based his book and therapeutic protocol: Acceptance, Abstinence, Congruency, and Practice. I had similarly developed four foundational principles of healing and growth when I developed Journey into Manhood in 2002: Masculinity, Authenticity, Needs fulfillment, and Surrender, or what we call M.A.N.S.® principles. Terry and I were both struck by the intersecting truths we had separately uncovered.

I have always believed that truth shows up in many different places and is reinforced in many different ways—but that it is always congruent with biblical truths. That is what Terry and I have found in following our separate calls to "strengthen our brothers."

I believe that you will recognize the truth and feel the hope that Terry and Scott share with you in *Walk by Faith Not by Sexuality* if you will listen with your heart as well as your mind. The principles they teach, if followed authentically, have the power to change lives.

Rich Wyler

Founder and Director

Brothers on a Road Less Traveled ("Brothers Road")

Overview

Audience: We wrote this book primarily for Christian men of faith who experience same-sex attractions that do not align with their deeply held values and beliefs. We also hope this book will bring wives, parents, brothers and sisters, friends, church leaders and fellow congregants some much-needed understanding, clarity, and compassion on this complex and difficult issue. We want to come alongside those who have struggled to feel accepted by the church because of their sexuality. In addition, this book presents a model for congregations to stay true to biblical principles while actively supporting healing for the men in their church.

Goal: The goal of this book is to help men align their values with their same-sex attraction (SSA) experience and find inner peace, and perhaps the byproduct is to begin boasting about their weakness. As 2 Corinthians 12:9–10 notes, "And He said to me, My grace is sufficient for you, for power is perfected in weakness. Most gladly, therefore, I will rather boast about my weaknesses, so that the power of Christ may dwell in me. Therefore, I am well content with weaknesses, with insults, with distresses, with persecutions, with difficulties, for Christ's sake; for when I am weak then I am strong."

Faith-Based Acceptance, Abstinence, Congruency, and Practice

Therapy is a Christian-based, biblically congruent protocol developed for Christian leaders and faith-based counselors. These biblical principles help conceptualize how to apply the guidance woven throughout Scripture to those struggling with sexual incongruency while seeking alignment with their faith.

Note: Scriptural references throughout are from the New American Standard Bible (NASB) 1995.

ACCEPTANCE

God loves and **accepts** us just as we are!
(Romans 15:7; 1 Timothy 1:15)

ABSTINENCE

God calls us to **abstain** from fleshly lusts,
which wage war against the soul.
(1 Peter 2:11; 1 Thessalonians 4:3)

CONGRUENCY

God calls us to live in **congruency** by confessing
our struggles and sharing our burdens.
(Acts 19:18; 2 Corinthians 12:9-10)

PRACTICE

God calls us to **practice** (not to perfect)
truth, light, and righteousness.
(John 3:21; 1 John 3:7)

Table of Contents

CHAPTER 1

"And Such Were Some of You"[1]

HI, I'M TERRY.

I am a Board-Certified Professional Christian Counselor who specializes in treating addictions and trauma. I also offer Christian counseling and mentoring to those who experience distress over same-sex attractions that conflict with their faith and values. Approximately half of my caseload is working with couples, and I am one in a pool of therapists available to students in need of counseling at a Christian university. If asked to state my sexuality in one sentence: I am a heterosexual male who is faithful to my wife, and I have a bisexual arousal template.

Throughout my lifelong journey, incongruent sexual feelings did not align with my Christian values until I really began paying attention to what the Bible had to say on the subject. When I truly listened to Scripture, while ignoring what culture and even some in the church were teaching, I found peace. God loves me deeply just as I am (Romans 8:38–39) while calling me—and all of humanity—toward a deeper spiritual plain.

Many in society may view sexual orientation and an arousal template as inseparable, and in some ways, they are. However, there are cultural considerations that impact one's lived experience. An arousal template can be different from a person's identified sexual orientation. An arousal template is a set of characteristics that someone may find to be captivating. It can include types of sexual activities, body features (feminine/masculine), body parts, situations, places, or even storylines that one finds to be alluring.

Sexual orientation is often how a person identifies within a culture (heterosexual, homosexual, bisexual, pansexual, etc.) as an indication of how a person may be living out his or her life within relationships or sexual expression. An individual can have a bisexual arousal template while identifying as, and living as, heterosexual within their culture. This is my lived experience.

For me and many others whom I have come to know, incongruent sexual feelings have created lifelong internal conflicts, isolation, and even deep-seated emotional wounds.

As a teenager and young adult, I experienced the internal conflicts between an ever-increasing hypersexualized culture and a faith community that is often silent or critical on issues of sexuality. This led me down the path of self-destruction and addiction. After hitting bottom in 2001, I began a journey of seeking greater understanding and self-acceptance. I began coming to terms with my sexuality. I began being open about it while living congruently with my faith. I began celebrating my salvation rather than my sexuality, which wasn't easy, but God has opened doors I never thought possible.

I began working with my dear friend Scott, who serves as an evangelist. Together, we developed a therapeutic protocol to conceptualize spiritual, emotional, and sexual journeys like mine within a biblical framework. We have summarized the path by focusing on the Scriptural principles of **acceptance** (accepting God's will, accepting ourselves, and receiving His acceptance of us), **abstinence** (from acting on same-sex desires), **congruency** (being authentically known), and **practice** (righteous living). Thus, we have come to call this protocol Faith-Based Acceptance, Abstinence, Congruency, and Practice Therapy (FB-AACP).

As we developed this framework, along the way we encountered four "M.A.N.S.® principles" of Masculinity, Authenticity, Needs fulfillment, and Surrender, as taught by the nonprofit community called Brothers Road (www.brothersroad.org), with which I have found a particular affinity. Together, the FB-AACP pillars and the M.A.N.S. principles have helped me to live authentically and in harmony with my faith, values, beliefs, and life goals.

In short, FB-AACP Therapy is about biblical sexual integrity. I have met many people from all walks of life and differing backgrounds who follow this same formula as their lived experience. Knowing these courageous people has been a blessing.

The problem with applying "Band-Aid healing" to bullet-wound issues is that those wounds never fully heal. In my life, I sought help from well-intentioned people without ever giving them the opportunity to fully show up by knowing the full extent of my struggles. Why is that? Why did I have such fear of sharing my whole story? I always respect those who share their woundedness and humanity. It does take courage because doing so brings with it the risk of rejection. However, when it came to sharing my own story and struggles, I felt paralyzed.

Biblical Masculinity vs. Tyrannical Masculinity

1 COR 16:13-14

"Be on the alert, stand firm in the faith, act like men, be strong. Let all that you do be done in love."

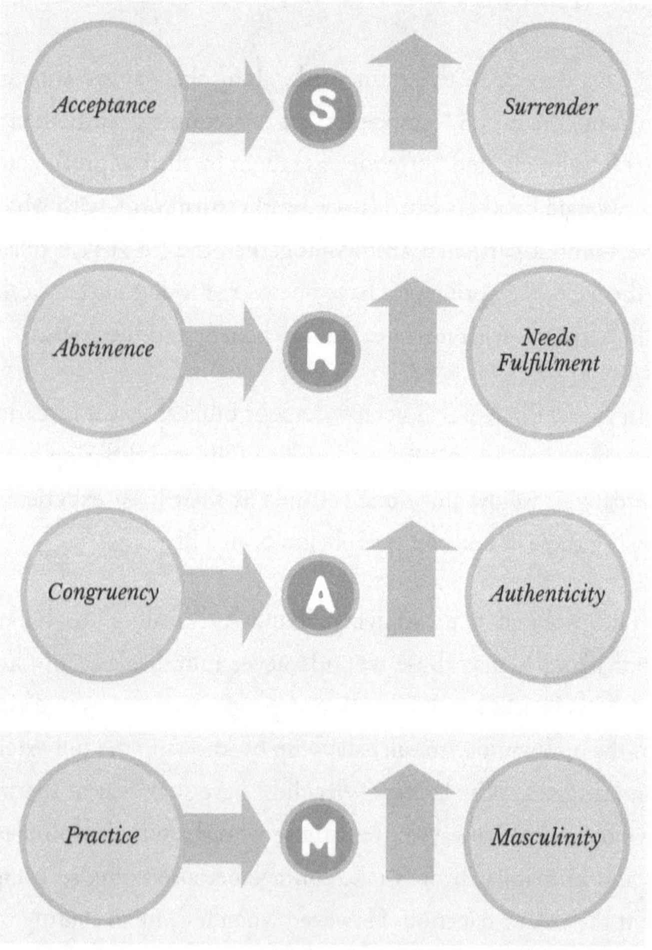

In 2004, while running on the treadmill at the gym in the U.S. Coast Guard Sault Ste. Marie's military base in Michigan, I watched the television news with great interest. A press conference was underway of the New Jersey governor resigning from office after admitting to an extramarital affair with another man. He stated, "At a point in every person's life, one has to look deeply into the mirror of one's soul and decide one's unique truth in the world, not as we may want to see it, or hope to see it, but as it is. And so, my truth is that I am a gay American. And I am blessed to live in the greatest nation with the greatest tradition of civil liberties in the world, in a country that provides so much to its people."[2]

I have thought about that press conference on many occasions, pondering my own truth. I had respect for the governor for openly stating his beliefs even though I see the world differently. If I were to stand in front of a podium today, I would say something like this: "I stand before you today with my wife, Holly, at my side. We stand as one flesh joined together by God's divine power. First and foremost, I share the truth about my life and experience to give voice to that golden child within who, years before, attempted to end his life. He cried out to the Lord and Savior, Jesus Christ, and the Lord answered the boy's call.

"The truth is that I am a heterosexual male with a bisexual arousal template. Regardless of this truth, God beckons me to His kingdom with great enthusiasm. There have been times in my life when I have desired nothing more than to throw myself into the pursuit of satisfying every form of sexual lust. However, I have searched God's word on such matters and sought His guidance. His words to me are clear: God loves and *accepts* me for who I am, but he calls me to *abstain* from lusts waging war against my soul, and He strengthens me to be *congruent* in my testimony while *practicing* righteousness.

"My wife knows my struggles with same-sex attraction and isn't bothered by them. I choose to live a heterosexual lifestyle, embracing my masculinity just as God designed me, while living in alignment with Scripture. These are my values. These are my beliefs. Living my life according to our Creator's instruction is most important to me because I realize this world is only temporary."

Hi, I'm Scott.

I have been a preacher of the gospel of Jesus Christ since 1999. I did not grow up in a religious home, but during high school, I came to understand that the Bible was more than a mere collection of religious writings and human ideals; it was a book that only God could write. Until I was introduced to the Bible through Jenna, the woman who would eventually become my wife, I lived an irreligious life and struggled with the impact that a selfish existence has upon all of us. I believed the myth that the Bible and religion were based upon faith, and that anyone reasonable or aware of modern science would disregard it. It was only once I came to see the evidence and the reasonable nature of Christianity that I accepted the Bible for what it is—God's Word.

My wife Jenna and I have been married 23 years (as of 2023) and have eight children. We have been blessed to grow our family through adoption. Through that process, we have come to learn many lessons about life, trauma, and the difficulties that life without God can have on adults and children alike.

I've been blessed to be able to dedicate the last two decades of my life to preaching and teaching the Bible both publicly and privately. I have seen time and again through my evangelism and counseling that the messages of the Scriptures work. We are designed by God, and the Bible is His instruction manual for living. When we ignore it, we become broken, dissatisfied, and helpless. When we return to our Creator and trust His plan, He can take us from depths of hopelessness to heights of restoration and purpose we never thought possible.

Terry and I met during my time preaching in Monroe, Washington. I consider Terry a wonderful friend and am happy to offer a biblical worldview to his therapeutic protocol. The ideas Terry has implemented in his therapy to help those struggling with same-sex attraction or sexual incongruency are clearly seen in the Scriptures. The early church dealt with many of the same humanistic and sexually charged cultural problems that ours does today, and God gave them the tools and patterns to accept where they were: abstain from what was sinful, speak honestly of what they had been through, and practice a new life in Jesus the Christ. This should be of great comfort to us today. As Solomon said in the book of Ecclesiastes 1:9, "There is nothing new under the sun." Today's problems are human problems, and human problems can be redeemed with God's guidance.

Terry's struggles are all too common. Unfortunately, the most surprising aspect of Terry's journey is that he didn't give up. Far more often in this hypersexualized culture, young men and women are experiencing deeply traumatic things at a very young age, encountering sexual situations far too young, and growing up in deeply unstable households. Because of these experiences, many of them are turning away from God instead of drawing toward Him.

The culture we live in is busy turning morality upside down. This cultural-social experiment matches the words of Isaiah 5:20: "Woe to those who call evil good, and good evil; Who substitute darkness for light and light for darkness; Who substitute bitter for sweet and sweet for bitter!"

Marriage is exchanged for cohabitation without commitment, divorce is rampant, vows are broken, sexual abstinence is scorned while unfettered sexual exploration is encouraged—and the results are in. We are less happy, less committed, and less at peace. The social experiment of life without God at the center is a complete failure, and children who eventually become adults are left carrying the burden of life without a good foundation.

The culture we live in is faith-inhibiting. To be a Christian who lives by their convictions and chooses to *abstain from sin (sin that is often pleasurable in the short-term) for the sake of our faith in Jesus is ridiculed. Finding a therapy with a faith-based worldview is often discouraged, and true healing is inhibited because of it.*

Sexually "deviant" behavior (deviant meaning behavior that deviates from God's plan for traditional marriage and complementary gender roles) is celebrated in society today. The humanistic culture of today demands more than just acknowledgment; it demands affirmation ... this poses a very real problem for the Christian struggling with same-sex attraction.

Christians with same-sex attractions recognize what the Bible says about homosexuality, and like all humans, they also deeply yearn for community and affirmation. The Bible offers another option: building acceptance and community within the church through acknowledgment of the individual and praise of their efforts toward abstinence. It is honorable to acknowledge one's struggles and it should be honored amongst God's people! Can the church build a sense of community so that those struggling with SSA do not feel isolated, but acknowledged and embraced as they seek to follow God's will? I believe they can.

This is not a new problem.

The life of Samson in Judges 13–16 is an excellent example of the struggle with sexual sin that happens when people feel lonely. Samson's life is a living proverb on what happens to far too many. Samson's life is a story of loneliness. He fights a lonely war as a solitary soldier, without friends, without companions, and is rejected by even his own countrymen. His life is socially distanced to the max.

This isn't an excuse for Samson's behavior, but the Bible does lay out a clear explanation of how he got to the stage of his life for which he is most well-known. Samson, in this loneliness, becomes a womanizer. He visits harlots, he wanders from one sexual encounter to another, and eventually he gets caught in the web of a woman named Delilah who leverages his lonely love-seeking heart to trap him and destroy him.

If you read Samson's life carefully, you will see the story of a young man who grows up without many healthy relationships and then makes bad choices trying to fill a void in his heart. His behavior isn't acceptable, but it is understandable. So many men and women are living Samson's lives, using sexual sin to replace emotional trauma, but the hole just gets bigger instead of being filled.

This is where the church comes in. God's people are meant to help re-establish healthy relationships in the lives of those who have been damaged by sin, trauma, and poor guidance during childhood. Older men are to become father figures to younger men (see 1 Timothy 5:1), and older women are to encourage younger women to embrace their God-given femininity (see Titus 2:3–5). The church is meant to work like an organism, a body, to send energy to heal the wounds of the various parts and strengthen them (see Ephesians 4:15–16). However, this is hard to do if the church does not take an active role in embracing the wounded.

Unfortunately, while the culture is busy talking openly about sexual desires, promiscuity, and every possible facet of sensuality, the Lord's people are very hesitant to speak openly. I suspect this is for multiple reasons. One reason is a sense of modesty and decorum—God's people value the intimacy of the sexual relationship and are tired of it being treated as a commonplace topic by the world. We wish to treat it as sacred and honored (see Hebrews 13:4). This desire to avoid lewd speech or sensationalism can lead us to not talk about the topic at all. This is a mistake.

Another reason is shame. The data is clear that pornography usage and sexual deviancy are problems among religious people, too. It is not just those outside of Christ who are being trapped in sexual sin; the snares of the devil have infiltrated the computer screens and bedrooms of Christians, too. Without confession, there is no healing, and without healing, those who should be prepared to openly help the next generation are still silently suffering with their own regrets, shame, and guilt. Hidden sin creates multi-generational problems.

However, it doesn't have to be this way. God's people have a roadmap, through the Scriptures, to defeat sexual sin and openly accept forgiveness. When fornication, adultery, and homosexuality were called out in the Corinthian church by the apostle Paul, he openly affirms, "Such were some of you" (see 1 Corinthians 6:9–11).

This means that the church in Corinth was aware of these sins in more than just an abstract way existing within the culture—they personally knew Christians who had successfully repented of those sins and were now pursuing a life of abstinence from sin, peace with God, and a practiced faith. This is no small thing! This meant that on any given Sunday, someone struggling with same-sex attraction, fornication, etc., would be able to recognize that someone else in the pew had struggled and prevailed against the very sins that were currently haunting them. Those in the battle could be openly mentored by those who had already claimed victory.

The Scriptures provide that path to full recovery from sexual sin and a life that is congruent with both where you have been and where you are going. In Christ, there is both hope and redemption. The church should provide that sense of community to those seeking acceptance, willing to abstain, claim their place in God's kingdom, and practice His ways.

CHAPTER 2

- - - - - - - - - - - - - - - - - - - -

"And They Laughed Him to Scorn"[3]

THE YEAR WAS **2006.** MY WIFE, HOLLY, AND I HAD BEGUN attending the Monroe Valley Church of Christ a few months prior to my deployment. Holly and I came from a denominational religious background, but neither of us had any real biblical knowledge. All we knew was that our past emotional wounds drew us toward wanting to know God. Recent newlyweds with a newborn on the way, we felt belonging to a church community would be helpful in our prospective journeys of recovery. The love we had for each other was strong and pure. When Holly and I were dating, I shared with her my struggles with my sexuality. I thought it would scare her away, but it only drew us closer together.

My addiction to alcohol went through a 10-year incubation period prior to hitting bottom at the age of 29. During that period, I lived a life of excess and promiscuity until near destruction. It seemed like Holly could not have been less bothered by my past. The same was true for me. Holly battled her own demons revolving around an eating disorder and abusive relationships. While we both brought to the relationship shadows of shame, we loved how we saw ourselves reflected in each other's eyes.

We had stumbled upon the church on a whim, but it was a Godsend. Holly had never lived anywhere other than her hometown in the state of Wisconsin. As recent transplants to the state of Washington, we knew I had a six-month deployment on the horizon. Living across country from family, Holly would have little support raising our newborn. However, the bonds we formed with the members of the church in such a short time were a blessing. At the church, a new preacher named Scott had just joined the congregation. Little did I know that Scott (the coauthor of this book) would be pivotal in my lifelong journey of recovery. When the time came to deploy, Holly and I were both comforted by the support we had from the church.

Holly and I kept in touch via emails and phone calls throughout the deployment, which was a traumatic time for us both. To prevent her from worrying, I refrained from sharing the intense struggles I was having.

Back home after completing the six-month patrol circumnavigating the globe in an extremely toxic work environment, I sought out Scott's spiritual counsel for help treating what I would come to learn was post-traumatic stress disorder (PTSD). As I sat across the kitchen table from Scott in his home one day, flashes of the deployment crossed my mind like a ticker tape in a continuous loop.

I explained to him how I was responsible for briefing the ship's command on operations daily, and as a result, I was continually in the commanding officer's (CO's) line of fire. (The CO of a ship is also called the captain.)

As one senior officer later wrote in support of my claim for PTSD, "The captain frequently reacted with extreme anger and even violence to insignificant events beyond the crew's control. He would grab crewmembers or brace up as though he were about to punch them. He would smash phone receivers to bits, personally threaten and humiliate crewmembers, throw objects at or near crewmembers, and more. We never knew what would set him off, and nearly everyone onboard was terrified of having to give him bad news, or even to be near him when someone else did. We lived in fear every minute of every day, and people hid from the captain, or hid the truth from him, whenever possible."

On one occasion, there was a minor miscommunication between the helicopter pilot and the ship during a training exercise at sea where the pilot had allegedly flown within an unsafe distance from our carrier, though we were simulating fog on a perfectly clear day. No one was ever in actual danger, so it should only have resulted in a calm discussion about how to prevent a repeat of the situation. But the captain exaggerated the situation and used it to humiliate me in front of the crew.

With the ship's senior leadership and crew huddled around the chart table, I was providing the logistics for the morning's preflight brief. The captain stopped me mid-sentence. "We all know what the problem is here, Chief!" he barked at me. "It's you! You're fired!"

Everyone's eyes were fixed on me in silent shock. In an arrogant and sanctimonious faction, the captain had just fired me, the division chief of the Combat Information Center, from my collateral duty as Air Direction Controller. Standing there in disbelief, I seemed to be having an out-of-body experience. The humiliation and shame were palpable. There were about 20 to 25 junior and senior members of the ship's crew crowded into the center. The captain finished up with his tirade and stormed out. I could see people whispering and talking, and some were openly snickering, turning away with glances in my direction.

While I continued carrying out my regular daily duties, this humiliation became seared in my memory. Traumatically, it was the first of many more to come before my deployment ended.

Scott responded with compassion and affirmation. Yet what I didn't tell him—I was at the time too ashamed to tell him—was that my trauma response to the captain's treatment of me was partially because that new humiliation on the ship had echoes of another humiliation decades earlier.

It was when I was just 13 years old. At that time, it was common for my friends to congregate at Larry's house after school. Hanging out in his room smoking cigarettes was a regular pastime for our small group. One day, we were in Larry's bedroom chatting about the day's events with our friends Brian, Tony, and Steve. While lying on the floor, I felt myself get an erection (which I didn't realize at the time was such a common experience for teenage boys). I was mortified. How could this happen now? I made the decision to stand quickly and go to the bathroom to relieve the discomfort.

Returning to the room, I sat back down. I noticed my friends averting direct eye contact while laughing. Tony began to ask me questions like, "Do you like Michael Jackson's song 'Beat It'?"

Everyone laughed; Larry lifted a pillow to his face, attempting to hide his laughter. The implication was clear, and I was mortified. They had obviously noticed my arousal and guessed that I had gone to the bathroom to masturbate. What made it so much worse was that when the topic of masturbation had come up in the past, many of my friends had associated the act itself with being gay, so I was sure they would spread a rumor that I was gay throughout the school.

Consumed with shame and fear, I said I had to leave. I raced home, dropped my bike in the front yard, and went straight to the bathroom. Looking in the mirror, I swallowed an entire bottle of Comtrex, a potent cold medicine, in the hopes it would end my life. Hours later, I woke with the worst headache imaginable. Regrettably, I was still alive.

This event occurred on a Friday afternoon, kicking off Christmas vacation in the eighth grade. The shame and fear did not lessen. I resolved that I was not going back to school. For the next two weeks, I remained at home, isolated, planning another suicide attempt. Had we owned a firearm, I surely would have used it. Consumed with shame and fear of public humiliation, I tried stabbing myself in the gut several times. I lost weight. My sister noticed and asked me to lift my shirt. I refused, knowing that she would see the many puncture wounds in my stomach. I just could never bring myself to fully impale the knife.

I wrote several suicide letters expressing my love for family and friends without explaining the reason. I was terrified that my friends would brand me as being gay (if it was not circulating around the neighborhood already) for suspecting that I had masturbated in Larry's bathroom. As the days ticked past, the time came for me to return to school. I had to inform my mother. I told her what had happened and about the attempts to end my life. She demanded to see the suicide letters that I had written, which I produced. Shattered, my mother frantically sought out a child psychologist and scheduled an appointment.

Unfortunately, out of shame and fear of how Scott would react, I never shared this foundational trauma experience with Scott until 16 years later.

CHAPTER 3

"Delivered From the Power of Darkness"[4]

As **D**r. **H**ovsapian entered the waiting room, my mind was in a haze. His kind voice shocked me out of my thoughts. He introduced himself to my mother and me. He was a shorter, heavier version of Mr. Rogers. I stood to follow him to his office while my mom remained in the waiting room. I was not going to tell him the whole truth, just enough to get me through the current crisis. Dr. Hovsapian buzzed us through the hospital doors. We entered his office, and I sat down.

The truth was that while lying on the floor in Larry's bedroom, I had become aroused when he took off his shirt. When I went to the bathroom, I quickly masturbated while thinking about him. I grew up attracted to the opposite sex but discovered same-sex attraction after hitting puberty.

After meeting with Dr. Hovsapian, I was stabilized but still so scared of the mockery that surely awaited me when I returned to school. I was allowed to stay home from school for another week.

The Friday before I had to return to school, I finally cried out to Jesus. I asked for His help while speaking to His image on a pamphlet that I had found on my mother's dresser. I do not recall the exact words that were written on the pamphlet, but it was written in the first person, as if coming directly from Jesus Himself. It read something like, "If you are in need, ask for My help. I will hear you. And, for the rest of your life, when you're in distress, cry out to Me. I will never leave you nor forsake you."

With tears streaming down my face, I prayed, "Jesus, please, please help me!"

In that instant, one of my friends from that fateful afternoon in Larry's bedroom called, inviting me outside to play. Startled that he would even want to, I reluctantly agreed. We met up with the other friends who had been in the room that day, the ones who had snickered and laughed. I braced myself for the worst—but not one of them ever mentioned the event again. It was as if Christ completely erased it from existence. It felt like a miracle had occurred, and for me, it had.

I continued to meet with Dr. Hovsapian for three years. The sessions were extremely helpful. But out of shame and fear of his reaction, I never shared the whole story with respect to my attraction to Larry.

As an adult many years later, my "body memory"[5] of that childhood event rippled underneath the surface as I stood there in the Combat Information Center. My childhood shame was re-triggered by the new trauma, thus amplifying the shame of being fired. The flashback to my childhood sexual confusion and shame, combined with being viewed as incompetent, was excruciating.

During the patrol, the stress became so unbearable that I reached out via email to that young preacher, Scott, whom I'd met at church shortly before my deployment. Simply communicating the events to another person outside the ship was a relief. Scott would suggest Bible verses to consider while offering practical advice. He was much like a spiritual wartime conciliar until returning home.

At the end of my deployment, sitting across from Scott and processing the events of the previous six months was more therapeutic than our email exchanges had been. He understood the daily cycle of humiliation and retribution made worse by an untenable watch rotation.

The watch rotation had been six hours on, six hours off. This continued for months, which meant I could never sleep more than a few hours at a time, and even then, only if our "off" time was outside of the regular workday. I was so far beyond the point of exhaustion that I was prone to mistakes, even though I was terrified of the retribution that would result from the slightest misstep.

Returning home, I discovered that insomnia was a byproduct of this sustained, untenable work schedule while under duress. This insomnia would plague me for years. It was like having the gas pedal of a car pressed down to the floor. Even when the foot comes off the gas, the pedal can get stuck with the engine still revving unnecessarily.

I later learned that the CO was eventually relieved of his command for assault on another crew member, but the damage I had experienced under his watch was already done. My sense of masculinity eroded with each instance of his berating with the precision of a sociopath highly attuned to causing psychological torment. This, coupled with the knowledge and shame of my life-long struggle with same-sex attraction, left me feeling devastated.

Visiting with Scott was my second episode of counseling (my sessions with Dr. Hovsaipian being the first). Intertwined with the trauma from the patrol was the internal conflict of secrecy. During the patrol, I coped with the stress with a strange mixture of prayer and sexual fantasy. I prayed for God's strength daily—but also fantasized about members of both sexes. This internal duplicity added to my self-hatred and loathing. As in my counseling years before, I did not intend to share the whole truth with Scott. I was grateful that I could process the patrol, but I had no intention of ever sharing my sexual struggles.

I should add here that while my arousal template is bisexual, I do not identify as such. For me, my faith outweighed my sexuality, and I could never be comfortable living a bisexual lifestyle. I believe God's word concerning His perspective that same-sex relations are outside of His plan for healthy relationships, as noted in the books of Romans chapter 1, 1 Corinthians chapter 6, and Galatians chapter 5.

For these reasons, I locked away this part of my identity to the world. I later learned that not being known for who I really am while also harboring shameful thoughts created intense stress.

CHAPTER 4

"Deliver Me from All Distress"[6]

"Same-sex attraction is not our enemy. It's not a battle to fight or a cross to bear. It doesn't require a 'cure.' SSA can be our teacher. It may have much to reveal to us about ourselves, our unmet needs, or unhealed wounds" (www.brothersroad. org, 2022).

JAY STRINGER, AUTHOR OF THE BOOK *UNWANTED*, EXPLAINS HOW an arousal template has links to our past. In one interview, he shared that he often asks his clients to have a conversation with their arousal template while enjoying a cup of coffee on the front porch. In 2022, I attended Jay's *Unwanted* Guide Training with six other therapists, and it was so helpful to my healing. Jay wrote in a recent correspondence titled, "Our Sexual Story is Not Random":

The sexual story we find ourselves within is not random. It is shaped by the views of sex we inherit from our families and communities, the beautiful and adverse experiences our bodies undergo, our partners, and what we choose to give our sexual attention to. Yet so few of us have ever been invited or asked to explore our sexual story.

One thing that might surprise you is that our sex life is shaped by our earliest attachment. When people experience stress, trauma, and emotional abandonment early in life, their endorphin systems (which facilitate attachment) do not fully develop. So, when people use a substance like alcohol, heroin, or porn, it can feel like a warm hug or a rush of pleasure they have never fully known. Therefore, rather than trying to fight against a behavior you don't want, fight to extend kindness and connection to the parts of your story that are hurting.

These words ring true to me as I examine my own sexual story.

As an adolescent, my older brother Gary terrorized me with his explosive temper, physical abuse, and bullying. When he was upset with me, he would shove, punch, or threaten me into silent submission. By that age, Gary was already 6'3" while I was 5'8". I hated that nature had cheated me out of size.

I can recall demoralizing scenes when my brother would get upset, dragging me in the living room with a fistful of my hair, plugging his nose and blowing his snot on me, being cornered in a room while doing my best to protect myself from punches. There were verbal threats of violence when my parents were not looking. "Wait until we are alone," he would mouth, leaving me with an impending sense of doom. Walking with my father in the mall, my brother would look at me with his cinched-up face, intently staring while quickly mouthing, "You're dead."

When I was seven, my parents divorced. Without my father around, my brother became even bolder. Sitting in the back seat with him while driving to St. Louis for vacation was tormenting. On one occasion, my mother became lost, which enraged him. He punched the seat between us repeatedly, then stared at me in the hopes that I would give him any reason to lash out at me. My mother's interventions did little to control him.

The worst memory was when we were visiting relatives in Minnesota. I was downstairs with my niece helping her get ready in the bathroom. My niece was sitting on the sink vanity. My brother burst into the bathroom. He pointed at her face, threatening and snarling. The night prior, he was high on cocaine in the next-door neighbor's yard, so we learned. My niece could not have been more than five years old. He pointed at her face shouting, "Why did you tell them where I was, you little bitch? You keep your mouth shut." Then he slapped her in the face.

I froze. The words that came out of my mouth brought up a sense of shame and cowardice. All I did … the only word that would come out of my mouth was a weak "Garrry!" My older sister (my niece's mother) burst into the bathroom and pushed our brother hard. He flew backward. I picked up my niece and turned her away from what was happening. My sister pushed my brother again very hard. He flew backward again … still with a face of anger but withering away, backing down. My older sister was fearless and strong. She was a shorter athlete in height, but the two of them weighed about the same. Had my brother attempted to fight back, I'm sure he would have lost, as she presented like a fierce bear protecting her cub.

But for me, there was a constant feeling of walking on eggshells as a child. As an adult, I never allowed my brother to meet my wife or my children. I loved my brother in spite of the abuse, but after living through it, I would not allow him anywhere near my own family.

My brother passed away from an alcohol use disorder several years back, at the age of 50. I don't judge him for having developed that disorder. Except for the grace of God, I might have had the same fate. He called me on occasion when we were adults. He complained about our abusive father (without acknowledging his own abuse toward me), which is where my brother inherited his temper and propensity for violence.

He jokingly apologized on the phone at some point for being a terrible brother. He was always drunk when he called, so the conversations felt empty, void of any true reflection or change. I know he spent his adult life in torment, angry at the world, in and out of treatment centers, prisons, or mental health institutions. Like me, he was a product of our father's abuse—along with our own choices. After my parents' divorce, I longed deeply for a father, a male role model, and a stable home. My brother wasn't equipped, of course, to step into that role. In fact, his physical abuse toward me only increased. Throughout my life, I prayed he would find his own healing, but sadly, he never found his way out of the grips of his addiction. That could have been me.

Against this backdrop of experiencing a physically and emotionally abusive father and brother, my initial heterosexual arousal template became challenged over time as I longed for male acceptance, affection, and belonging.

All through my adolescence, I had crushes on girls who lived on my block or in grade school. I remember my first kiss with

Jenny in my basement, and my crushes on Carolyn, Kasha, and others. However, my longing for a positive male role model, male support, or coaching would eventually become unintentionally eroticized.

Shortly after my parents' divorce (when I was eight or nine), I was beating my next-door neighbor in a wrestling match in his front yard. His father came out of the garage and was watching us. We were just playing, laughing, and having fun … until his dad called him over and whispered in his ear. When Brian walked back to continue the match, I wouldn't reengage; I went home in tears.

I remember sobbing uncontrollably when I entered the house. I thought, "Brian has a father, a good father, a healthy father, a loving and caring father. I have an abusive father who left the home with an even more abusive brother tormenting my life."

The next day, I asked Brian what his dad had told him when he called him over. His dad advised him to tickle me, that's it. Nothing sinister, but he had a dad who was in his corner. The fact that I had no father (or brother) in my corner hurt so deeply.

After hitting puberty, my friend Mike and I wrestled in his pool after we had seen the movie *Superman II*. We were fake punching each other, wrestling, taking turns playing the role of Superman fighting off Zod and the others from the planet Krypton who had escaped their glass jail cell that brought them to Earth. It was this moment when a bisexual gene was engaged or flipped. Perhaps it was the mixture of play violence, camaraderie, and companionship. We were best friends. I realize now that the void of male approval that I longed for was strangely being eroticized through physical, playful interaction with my friend. I resisted these feelings, but they were there.

As I've explored my arousal template, "interviewing" it over a cup of coffee on how it came to be, as the author Jay Stringer suggested, it shared these memories with me for insight. No judgment. No condemnation. Just insight.

Everyone's story is different. As a therapist who treats sex addiction, I have sat with countless others who experience lightbulb moments when they gain insight into their arousal templates. In the workbook *The Seven Pillars of Freedom* by Pure Desire Ministries, there is an assignment where group members write down their sporting, financial, achievement, and sexual fantasies, and then compare them to discover the similarities.

There is a saying that all roads lead to Rome. Well, my fantasies all led to Rome in one path—I long to be desired, affirmed, wanted, and accepted (that is, loved). It plays out in my mind everywhere, and having had an abusive father and brother, it became the kindling that only needed a spark to trigger same-sex attraction. Belonging and acceptance is what I experienced in the pool with my friend—and the opposite of what I had experienced from my father and brother.

Sexual interests are not random, as they are often replaying or hoping for a different outcome, an unfulfilled desire. Or they are related to earlier events in life that were nurturing, so the individual continues to return to those (Roberts, 2021).

We all fantasize (daydream) about all sorts of things. I fantasize about a company calling to recruit me for an amazing job opportunity, or some government entity trying to talk me into joining the team. I fantasize about playing golf with friends who are eagerly wanting to engage me in conversations, and everyone looking on with admiration as I hit the ball with power. I fantasize about unfettered wealth to be able to bless those around me so I can be adored.

Likewise, my sexual fantasies involve being wanted, affirmed, admired, and sought-after by both women and men, until I'm powerless to resist.

When we understand others' histories, we can grow in Christlike compassion and acceptance of those who may "sin differently" than we do. Every story is different, but everyone has a story. As a church, we are called to bring healing balm to the wounded (and we are all wounded in one way or another) without judgment.

A Further Biblical Perspective (Scott)

When Terry first started talking to me back in 2006, we discussed the difficulties he had faced on the patrol, the frustrations of dealing with an incompetent and irrational commander, and the impacts it had on his personal life. But we never talked about the internal struggles Terry was having with his sexuality (same-sex attraction), fantasies, and his identity in Christ. He had shared that he was in recovery from an alcohol use disorder, but that was about the extent of what he disclosed from his past.

Holding back on the parts of our story that hold the greatest shame has a way of keeping us from actual healing. It is like doing half a root canal or partial removal of a cancerous tumor—the problem will just fester or manifest in new ways when we hold back. Getting to the bottom of unwanted behavior and emotional trauma can only be effective when the whole truth is shared. Healing is an all-or-nothing proposition. When we reach out for help, we are told to "confess [our] sins to one another and pray for one another that [we] may be healed" (James 5:16). As a friend and counsel to Terry, I wanted to help him, but I couldn't help him with what he didn't tell me. I wanted to pray for him, but I couldn't pray for what I didn't know. Partial confession often causes the person seeking help to feel less honest and more alone because they know they aren't sharing the whole truth about their struggles, temptations, sins, and heartache.

Healing isn't something you do by dipping your toe into the water. It is something you do by leaping off the cliff into the deep end. Jesus says in John 3:19–21 that one of the reasons people don't seek out the light of God is because they are afraid their own works will be exposed. "Exposed" is another word for "vulnerable." Vulnerability is hard, but it is necessary if we are going to truly become right with God. Avoiding the light provides temporary protection from the pain of dealing with trauma or sin, but it also creates a pattern of hiding that leads the person deeper and deeper into isolation. We are not meant to heal alone. We are not meant to isolate ourselves from others.

Over the years, I have talked with countless people about their lives, and it is typical for them to want to hold back. But healing doesn't happen until you open up. Honesty is a requirement for growth. When the truth is known by the right people who have the heart to help us, then we can be set free from the shackles of deception, fear, anxiety, and solitude. Part of the journey for every person dealing with sexual temptation—but, in particular, same-sex attraction—is reaching a point where they can be honest and open about where they are at.

Help begins with confession.

Without all the facts, even the best therapists, friends, mentors, or spiritual guides will be unable to provide good advice and guidance. So, my advice is this: If you are struggling, abandon half-measures. Be vulnerable to good people that you trust. And if you are in a position to be a friend, confidant, or guide to those with sexual struggles, ask questions, cultivate a character of trust and discretion, and praise honesty.

CHAPTER 5: THE ACCEPTANCE PRINCIPLE

"Accept One Another"[7]

EMBRACING REALITY AND OFFERING KINDNESS AND CONNECTION TO the painful aspects of my story started with acceptance. I sensed acceptance from God, as His Son had saved me when I cried out to Him as a young child. However, the greater struggle was achieving self-acceptance and finding acceptance within a community, and I later realized that these two were intimately intertwined. Romans 15:7 notes: "Therefore, accept one another, just as Christ also accepted us to the glory of God." These earlier verses in Romans 15:1–6 explain why this is important to God:

Now, we who are strong ought to bear the weaknesses of those without strength and not just please ourselves. Each of us is to please his neighbor for his good, to his edification. For even Christ did not please Himself; but as it is written, "The reproaches of those who reproached you fell on me." For whatever was written in earlier times was written for our instruction, so that through perseverance and the encouragement of the Scriptures we might have hope. Now may the God who gives perseverance and encouragement grant you to be of the same mind with one another according to Christ Jesus, so that with one accord you may with one voice glorify the God and Father of our Lord Jesus Christ.

1 Timothy 1:15 adds, "It is a trustworthy statement, deserving full acceptance, that Christ Jesus came into the world to save sinners, among whom I am foremost of all." In the verses preceding this verse (1 Timothy 1: 9–14), the apostle Paul discusses that the law (The Old Testament) was created for lawbreakers. But Paul was chosen to carry the good news of salvation through Christ (The New Testament) because he was a foremost sinner. No one is outside of God's redemption through his Son. No one.

I resonate with this quote from pages 417–418 of the "Big Book" of Alcoholics Anonymous. (The words and phrases in italics are my own additions.)

Acceptance is the answer to all my problems today. When I am disturbed, it is because I find some person, place, thing, or situation—some fact of my life—unacceptable to me, and I can find no serenity until I accept that person, place, thing or situation as being exactly the way it is supposed to be at this moment. Nothing, absolutely nothing, happens in God's world by mistake. Until I could accept my alcoholism *(and sexuality)*, I could not stay sober *(or congruent, or authentic, or at peace)*; unless I accept life completely on life's *(God's)* terms, I cannot be happy. I need to concentrate not so much on what needs to be changed in the world as on what needs to be changed in me and my attitudes.

So, it was with me. When I truly began accepting God's love for me and full acceptance of me, I began to change my life.

In 2016, I retired from the military after a combined 6 years in the U.S. Marine Corps Reserve and 20 years in the U.S. Coast Guard. I could have stayed in the service for another 10 years; however, I chose to pass up a promotion to Chief Warrant Officer 4 (a senior commissioned officer specializing in operations, in my case) and retired early. The money and prestige of rank meant nothing to me. I loved God and I wanted to start working as a therapist full-time.

Several friends whom I had served with throughout the years attended my retirement ceremony. None of them knew anything about my incongruent same-sex attractions. My friend, who was an agent with the Federal Bureau of Investigation, led the opening prayer, and another friend, who was a retired Lieutenant Colonel in the Marine Corps, gave the closing prayer. I was given a prestigious medal. A retirement-recognition letter from President Obama was read. I gave my speech. And with that, 26 years of service was over.

After retirement, what surprised me was how easy it was to leave it all behind. I had little interest in remaining connected to the friends I had made in the military. I think I now know why. The military served as a perfect mask (a cloak) to hide my incongruent sexual feelings. Working in a fast-paced, high-stakes environment, supercharged with testosterone, no one could possibly expect that I had a bisexual arousal template. *Terry couldn't possibly be gay.* And so it was that no one ever really knew me. Deep down, I felt like a poser, a fake, and a fraud.

Holly and I chose to retire to Appleton, Wisconsin. Following a couple of roles as a therapist at different clinics, I secured a position at the Veterans Administration (VA) as a Licensed Mental Health Professional Counselor. Before joining the VA, I perceived it as an extension of the military, but I was mistaken. The VA was established to provide physical and mental healing to those who served our country. Working with fellow veterans as they navigated their traumas eventually prompted me to seek a community referral to address my own military trauma.

I had attended training after training on various therapeutic protocols, all of which had value. In my third episode of care, I worked with a wonderful psychologist who helped me process the events of my military trauma, which eventually led back to my childhood trauma. I can recall when we first began discussing my same-sex attraction, just saying the words "same-sex attraction" created an intense fear of being discovered. I requested that he not include that part of my work in his clinical notes. We processed what had happened in Larry's bedroom. I had never shared that painful experience with my wife, Holly, and he encouraged me to do so. In hindsight, this advice was more powerful and transformative than I could have ever imagined.

During our dating days, I opened up to Holly about the places my alcohol addiction had led me, including some instances of same-sex encounters. However, I hadn't explicitly articulated those words. Tearfully, and burdened by shame, I had shared some of my experiences but hadn't delved into the extent of my bisexual attractions. At that point, I hadn't fully integrated that aspect of myself into my authentic life story, making it impossible at the time for me to have a truly candid discussion.

I was ready to change that now. Holly and I went on a weekend trip to Madison, Wisconsin, to celebrate our 16th wedding anniversary. As we drove to Madison, I was nervous about the trip because I knew I was finally going to put words to experiences. I was going to tell her about what happened in Larry's bedroom when I was a child and my subsequent suicide attempt. I was going to say out loud what I had never said before—that I have a bisexual arousal template.

I was uncertain what Holly's reaction would be. I didn't expect rejection because she had shown no signs of discomfort when I had shared aspects of my past during our dating days. My present discomfort stemmed from speaking the words out loud, "I have attractions toward men and women." However, I could assure her that despite these attractions, I've been a devoted, faithful, and loving husband, fully committed to honoring the vows we made before God on our wedding day.

At the hotel in Madison, as we lay in bed enjoying each other's company, I was finally ready to open up to her about my therapy work and the therapist's advice to discuss childhood events with her. I recounted the events of that crucial day in my friend's bedroom—my profound shame, my same-sex attraction, and my commitment to our marriage. Just like when we were dating, Holly responded with love and affection, showing no hesitation. Uttering those words aloud didn't seem to alter her feelings toward me at all. It was as if we were discussing any other topic. She didn't ask any questions or express concerns that I might act on those feelings. Our commitment to each other remained strong. In her eyes, and mine, we were made for each other by God.

The book of Ephesians chapter 5 discusses the unique characteristics of a husband and a wife:

> So, husbands ought also to love their own wives as their own bodies. He who loves his own wife loves himself; for no one ever hated his own flesh, but nourishes and cherishes it, just as Christ also does the church because we are members of His body. FOR THIS REASON, A MAN SHALL LEAVE HIS FATHER AND HIS MOTHER AND BE JOINED TO HIS WIFE, AND THE TWO SHALL BECOME ONE FLESH. This mystery is great; but I am speaking with reference to Christ and the church. Nevertheless, each individual among you also is to love his own wife even as himself, and the wife must see to it that she respects her husband.

After divulging my darkest childhood moments, shame, and lifelong struggles to Holly, I sensed a deep connection, as if we were one in a deeper way than we ever had been before. This newfound strength empowered me to embark on the journey of integrating my identity and being open about it to the world.

In American culture, the term "coming out" often implies accepting same-sex attraction and pursuing same-sex relationships. However, many Western mental health professionals endorse the psychological benefits of self-acceptance. It's important to recognize that the benefits of self-acceptance also extend to accepting one's sexual arousal template—while staying true to one's faith by abstaining from acting on same-sex attractions. And these psychological gains are just as significant.

In the spring of 2023, I was invited to speak at Florida College, a Christian university. During my presentation, with Holly in the front row, I offered a clinical overview of pornography addictions, discussed factors contributing to its cultural prevalence, and shared my personal experience with same-sex attraction. I also introduced resources for potential support groups on campus modeled after the successful Freedom Fighters groups here where we live in the Fox Cities area of Wisconsin. These groups consist of Christians who support each other in their journeys toward sexual integrity.

The presentation was promoted as a life-enrichment event, and attendance was optional. The goal for success was set for 25–50 attendees. Much to our surprise, 100–125 students filled the room, to the point where some even sat in the aisles. Additionally, 310 more people, most likely students, watched the presentation online. It's reasonable to estimate that nearly half of the student body tuned in. This was clear evidence to me of the hunger of so many young Christians to better understand and become better able to deal with issues related to pornography and same-sex attraction.

During the presentation, I had the opportunity to share my personal recovery story while showcasing a marriage filled with love and commitment. Having Holly by my side during the visit meant everything to me.

Students, eager to ask questions, surrounded us after the presentation, creating a vibrant atmosphere. Two psychology students specifically inquired about the dynamics of a marriage when there is an element of same-sex attraction. It was a thoughtful question.

In response, I emphasized that in a marriage with emotional intimacy and a sense of safety, there's no need to rush. We often engage in our deepest conversations while caressing each other in bed. Although spontaneous arousal may decrease in heterosexual relationships when one partner experiences same-sex attraction, and again later with age, responsive arousal tends to work just fine for us. In truth, our intimacy and emotional connection have increased with more frequent engagements in this manner. During intimacy, I feel as if the Holy Spirit is surrounding us. So, it's not only a physical or sexual experience but spiritual as well.

After my visit, I learned that two Freedom Fighters groups—one for men and one for women—have been established and are active on campus. Christians seeking support in their journey toward sexual integrity now have a battle plan and fellow peers to walk alongside them. This beautiful experience at the university marked a whole new level of self-acceptance for me. This never would have been possible had I not attended an experiential workshop called Journey into Manhood one year earlier.

On a warm summer day in Indiana, I had pulled up to a camp retreat for a weekend intensive presented by the Brothers Road organization—a "non-profit, multi-faith, international fellowship primarily of men from bisexual or same-sex-attracted backgrounds who—for (their) own, deeply personal reasons—typically do not accept or identify with the label 'gay' and prefer instead to explore and embrace (their) authentic masculinity" (www.brothersroad.org).

Walking up to the check-in table was surreal. Just by being here, these men knew my lived experience, and I knew theirs. While our stories and journeys differed, we shared a commonality that had caused untold distress throughout much of our lives.

As the weekend unfolded, I discovered something that I did not comprehend immediately. The weekend was focused not so much on our sexuality but around embracing and celebrating our authentic manhood.

I had spent a lifetime struggling with acceptance, which was always illusive. I had embraced manhood in artificial ways throughout my life via binge drinking, the military, and sexual exploration. Never had I been through a rite of passage into manhood guided by healthy men; men who knew my "shadow side" and who faced and shared their own.

I learned that the solution was to embrace masculinity, not shrink from it. Over the weekend, we challenged our unhealthy thinking about ourselves and our maleness and worked to develop our masculine traits, such as assertiveness, independence, initiative, decisiveness, and healthy risk-taking. We challenged ourselves by participating in masculinizing activities, surrendered false "gender imperatives" of what a "real man" was, and focused on similarities versus differences. In other words, we were challenged to see ourselves as equals to even the manliest of men.

At the intensive, I bonded as a brother with other men—finally feeling like "one of the guys." I engaged in inner-healing work addressing same-sex emotional wounds that had kept me from trusting other men. As a result, I found a meaningful male community for myself. For the first time in my life, I felt like a man among men!

For me, the challenge—and the need as a man with same-sex attraction—was to accept myself and let others know and accept me for who I truly am, not who I was pretending to be. This required me to embrace my own masculinity as an equal among other men. In my own case, it also required me to find fellow Christians who could not only hear and accept my walk, but also stand with me and celebrate me for my committed discipleship despite my unique challenges.

The church should be a tribe for the broken, but often, it only magnifies our isolation because of a perceived lack of safety in sharing who we really are. In Matthew 11:28–29, Jesus says, "Come to Me, all who are weary and heavy-laden, and I will give you rest. Take My yoke upon you and learn from Me, for I am gentle and humble in heart, and YOU WILL FIND REST FOR YOUR SOULS. For My yoke is easy and My burden is light."

As a therapist, I once sat with a client whom I'll call Dan. Dan suffered the isolation of being a man who experiences same-sex attraction yet chooses to live a heterosexual lifestyle. We walked through aspects of acceptance that seemed most important to him: acceptance by God, self-acceptance, and acceptance by others. He said that he felt 75% accepted by God, 20% accepted by himself, and 5% accepted by others.

I inquired what it would be like to belong to a congregation of Christians who knew he experienced same-sex attraction and supported his walk with Christ. He said he thought that acceptance by others (especially a congregation of Christians) would increase his feelings of acceptance by God and self into the 90% range. The next statement from Dan was disheartening. "But that does not exist," he said. "Christians view same-sex attraction as one of the worst sins imaginable."

Here was a man who loved God and loved his wife, but his arousal template included attraction toward men. He had consciously decided to abstain from activity that God determined to be outside of His design for sexual unions. It was a very manly choice, I might add. He could choose to live out his desires and be fully accepted, even celebrated by a large part of society, but instead he chooses to please God (abstaining because of his love for Him). I told him his choice to live his life in alignment with God's word was honorable. Impressive, even. It was not a leap to say that his choices were immensely pleasing to God.

Why would God's church not honor such men and women who make choices similar in nature? We do, you know. We honor those who—sometimes with great difficulty—abstain from alcohol, drugs, or any number self-destructive or sinful lifestyles. Why not honor those who abstain from acting out feelings of same-sex attraction or other sexually incongruent desires?

In his book *Facing the Shadows*, Dr. Patrick Carnes asserts that addiction stems from a failure of intimacy. He highlights the bonding process that takes place within Twelve Step communities. Driving this point home, Dr. Carnes discussed how Amnesty International worked to help victims of torture. Amnesty International made little progress in their attempts until they were able to connect victims of torture with other victims of torture. Only then did an acceptance of the experience take root.

Having been a member of Twelve Step support groups, I can attest to how beneficial they were to my own healing. However, in many church communities today there is little intimacy. We often know little about each other; therefore, the bonding process fails.

My motivation to go to church is to hear a message of God's word and partake in the Lord's supper (bread and fruit of the vine), which represents the body and blood of Christ. But in the back of my mind (even though I don't like to admit it) is a desire to look good. I wonder if those who regularly attend church these days are experiencing the greatest internal battles with their "shadow side." The inconvenience of getting dressed up on a Sunday morning, attending a formal service, and giving one's money suggests a need for connection and acceptance from God.

How powerful would this experience be if we were truly known by others, and we likewise knew them. The paradox is that when I know nothing of other's burdens or their wounds, and they know nothing of mine, I leave feeling disconnected, even alone. There is something missing, and I know it.

Acceptance is not an event. It is a process that takes place in the community. It is a process that the church could vastly accelerate if it truly embodied the message of Christ. A friend who is a high-level executive within a national sports team noted his desire to share his lifelong struggles with SSA with his pastor. He lamented, "I could never share my story because I don't think he could handle it."

Recounting sermons when the topic of homosexuality came up, his pastor had repeatedly expressed clear disdain for such struggles. How different would it be if he had preached the commonality with sexual struggles that we have all experienced, at some level, and the strength it takes to be known? How different would it be if he had preached how honorable and courageous it was to abstain from sexual behaviors outside of God's design?

This friend and I talked about the pillars of acceptance explored with my former client, Dan: God, self, and others. My friend said he felt 60% accepted by God, 80% accepted of himself, and 30% accepted by others. He shared that his self-acceptance was high due to his extensive work in therapy and his recent attendance at the Journey into Manhood intensive by Brothers Road.

I asked, "What would it be like if your pastor preached from the pulpit how honorable and courageous it was for those who experienced SSA to abstain from such practices out of their love for God?"

He replied, "It would change everything." His feelings of acceptance by God and self would increase into the 90% range, he said, while his feelings of being accepted by others would increase to 50%.

The nature of his hyper-masculine work environment created unique challenges to the possibility of believing that he would be accepted by others, but he felt if he were accepted in the church as courageous and honorable for the life choices he was making, it would eventually transcend into his professional life as well. In addition, my friend noted he would likely struggle less with lust and volunteer more of his time to the church.

In my heart of hearts, I know I am accepted by God—pursued even. The moment I spoke to Jesus as a 13-year-old boy, my life changed. I cannot explain it because, for me, it was a spiritual moment. I just know the presence of Christ was with me, loving me, accepting me—and He knew me, SSA and all. In later years, I chose to fall away, pursuing the cravings of the flesh. But when I listened, He was always calling me back to His light.

Even as a therapist who has engaged in extensive work over the years, I never felt safe in the church sharing my struggle with same-sex attraction as I strived to practice righteousness (right living). I felt that I would not be supported, accepted, or loved. I was so wrong.

In the chapter on congruency (chapter 11), I'll detail my experience of sharing my journey of same-sex attraction in the church. But for now, trust me, it was so healing. I feel members of the church are now more ready and willing to come alongside those who struggle with SSA than ever before. Faith communities do not need to shy away from preaching the teachings of God on matters of sexuality and the boundaries He has laid out for us. I have found in my own walk, God's teachings on such matters have been so helpful—lifesaving, in fact.

Recently, I worked with a couple on the topic of acceptance. Here are the husband's responses to questions I asked him to rate on a scale from 0–100:

Q: How much do you feel accepted by God?

A: 85%

Q: How much do you feel accepted by yourself (self-acceptance)?

A: 70%

Q: How much do you feel you would be accepted by your church if they knew your struggles?

A: 50%

I then asked, "If you belonged to a church who knew your struggles, and they accepted you 100%, with hearts of bearing one another's burdens, how would that impact your sense of self-acceptance and feelings of being accepted by God?"

He replied, "They would both change," adding, "I would feel 100% accepted by God and 100% accepted by myself if I felt accepted within my church after sharing my burdens."

Isn't that remarkable? This situation aligns with what the author Michael Dye (creator of the addiction-recovery program called the Genesis Process) and others refer to as a "double bind." It occurs when what we fear the most is also what we need the most.

After opening up about my struggles with same-sex attraction within the church and experiencing love and acceptance, I can confidently say that I feel 100% accepted by God, 100% self-acceptance, and 100% accepted by the church—all in accordance with His intended design.

CHAPTER 6

"Give Me Your Heart and Observe My Ways"[8]

By Scott Beyer

A Call to the Church

"But God demonstrates His own love toward us, in that while we were yet sinners, Christ died for us." (Romans 5:8)

One of the most difficult balances to strike in Christianity is to accept sinners while not accepting sin. It is much easier to exist in the world of extremes than to balance acceptance of sinners with a hatred of sin, yet the church must balance those things just as Jesus did.

Consider the scene found in Matthew 9. Jesus is invited to eat a meal at the house of Matthew, a well-known tax collector in the Galilean region of Israel. Jesus accepts Matthew's hospitality and eats with him. As Jesus reclines at the table, sinners of all sorts join the meal. Matthew had invited them as well. This is no small gathering; it is a large feast. Jesus freely intermingles with the tax collectors and sinners—speaking to them, connecting with them, and encouraging them in their efforts to follow Him and become His disciples. This open acceptance of sinners is met with rebuke from the religious parties of the day. Jesus' answer? "Those who are well have no need of a physician, but those who are sick. But go and learn what this means: 'I desire mercy and not sacrifice.' For I did not come to call the righteous, but sinners, to repentance." (Matthew 9:12–13)

The church is the extension of Jesus here on Earth. Christians are the hands, arms, legs, and feet of the Master (see 1 Corinthians 12:27). His work was to show mercy to sinners, not rejection. This requires proximity. We cannot help those who we keep at arm's length. Imagine a hospital that refused to see sick people, or a rescue squad that refused to respond to emergency calls for assistance. Proximity is a requirement to do the work of calling sinners to repentance—and that means we must accept people where they are so that we might help them get where God wants them to be.

Historically, some sins have carried with them a greater stigma than others. I call them "clean" and "unclean" sins. Of course, all sins are unclean—but we often feel more comfortable with sins like gluttony or laziness than with sins of the sexual realm. People openly talk about their struggles with overeating or procrastination without any fear of being rejected. These sins are considered acceptable by society even though the Bible is quite clear that gluttony and slothfulness are displeasing to God and harmful to man. If you need help with your diet, you can sign up for a support group, ask for support from your friends, publicly document your weight loss journey over social media, and receive praise for your successes and encouragement during your relapses. However, the same cannot be said about sexual struggles. Pornography addiction, same-sex attraction, promiscuity, and the journey to sexual purity often are battles fought in the darkness without support.

This is a problem. Sin needs to be brought to the light to be addressed. Pain must be spoken to be mended. Wounds cannot be healed in secret. Jesus makes it clear—proximity is the path of mercy.

Romans 15:7 says, "Therefore, accept one another, just as Christ also accepted us to the glory of God." We can accept people without accepting sin. Jesus proves that. If the church is going to do its job, we must make space for people to reach the Great Physician. Jesus ate meals with people while openly acknowledging them as sinners. When the Pharisees rebuked Jesus for eating with sinners, Jesus doesn't argue the goodness of those He is dining with, He acknowledges their sin, but also acknowledges their worth.

When Christians become a community that recognizes sin while also valuing souls, we become more evangelistic, more hopeful, and more biblical. If we wish to act like

Christ and seek to emulate first-century Christianity, there must be a restoration of love for all sinners, which means we must seek to find ways and pathways for "unclean" sins to be addressed with mercy and love. The church is intended to be a hospital for souls. All need to be welcome to the healing waters of Jesus.

So, how do we do that? First, we need to acknowledge that spending time with people is not the same thing as condoning sin. We can accept people without accepting sin. We've been trained to believe that acceptance involves suspending our views on morals and ethics, but that isn't accurate at all. Jesus was very clear on His views of right and wrong behavior. Jesus accepted people for the purpose of transforming them into His disciples. If the only place for acceptance is in the world, then people will seek out acceptance in a worldly environment. Those struggling with same-sex attraction need to know that they can be accepted by God's people as they strive to abstain from the passions of their flesh.

Which leads to the second thing we must do: Christians need to create space for repentance.

CHAPTER 7: SPIRITUAL SURRENDER[9]

Let God Have His Way In Your Heart

IN SUPPORTING SAME-SEX-ATTRACTED MEN IN RESOLVING INNER conflicts about their sexuality or arousal templates, the non-profit fellowship Brothers Road identifies four pillars of inner healing: Masculinity, Authenticity, Needs fulfillment, Surrender (M.A.N.S.). I'll discuss those pillars in reverse as they align with Acceptance, Abstinence, Congruency, and Practice.

Perhaps the most oft-repeated message of the Bible is God calling us to repent of our sins and return to Him, yielding our hearts to His will. In the language of Twelve Step addiction-recovery programs: We "made a decision to turn our will and our lives over to the care of God" (Step Three). We became "entirely ready to have God remove all (our) defects of character" (Step Six) and "humbly asked Him to remove our shortcomings" (Step Seven).

This "surrender principle" is likewise embraced by the Brothers Road program that I described earlier. Brothers Road describes surrender[10] in three broad categories:

1. Surrendering resistance to change
2. Yielding our will to God's will
3. Letting go of harmful thoughts and behaviors

While these principles were developed by the Brothers Road program to be applicable to all participants in their program, I have adapted them to be in the first person as they have applied so much to the path that I have walked.

SURRENDERING RESISTANCE TO CHANGE

Admittedly, this kind of inner journey has been, and is, an ongoing process. It's common to want the positive *results* of this healing work while at the same time being resistant—consciously or unconsciously—to do the hard work.

Sometimes, the hardest challenge for me is becoming aware of and directly facing my internal resistance to living my life according to the spirit in opposition to the flesh. Or thinking godly thoughts. Or moving outside my comfort zone. Internal resistance to change is always trying to protect myself from perceived danger or discomfort. It is necessary to consciously explore—with non-judgmental curiosity—the mental or emotional blocks that could be keeping me stuck. I have had to accept that resisting the temptations of the "natural man" is not easy. Apparently, God never intended it to be. But for me, it is worth it.

Likewise, I have had to stop living in the "shoulds" of what should be or should have been, or what people should do or should have done. I have learned to accept the world (often painfully so) as it is and work to let go of arguing with reality by wishfully thinking how I think the world *should* be.

Similarly, I have to continually reject the lie that I can find peace and wholeness through sin and rebellion against God's will. Neither can I find peace and wholeness by denying and suppressing the internal pain that so often causes me to turn to sinful or harmful behaviors. Rather, I continually (often through daily renewal) become willing to let God change me from within.

I have trained my mind to become ready to explore and address my inner conflicts and underlying pain as God's spirit searches the groaning of my soul when I'm in prayer. Romans 8:26–27 notes: "In the same way the Spirit also helps our weakness; for we do not know how to pray as we should, but the Spirt Himself intercedes for us with groanings too deep for words; and He who searches the hearts knows what the mind of the Spirt is, because He intercedes for the saints according to the will of God." Surrendering lust always brings my thoughts to Proverbs 5:1–6 which notes,

> My son, give attention to my wisdom, incline your ear
> to my understanding; that you may observe discretion and
> your lips may reserve knowledge. For the lips of an adulter-
> ess drip honey but in the end, she is bitter as wormwood,
> sharp as a two-edged sword. Her feet go down to death, her

steps take hold of Sheol. She does not ponder the path of life; Her ways are unstable, she does not know it.

YIELDING TO GOD'S WILL

The reality is that "self-will" (even in fantasy) inevitably leads me to discontentment when it goes up against God's will. The path to lasting change, in all areas of my life, has been a path of redirecting my thinking (my fears, my resentments, my desires, my lusts) to the gentle course corrections to be in alignment with God. And as often as I have asked God, he continually rescues me from my own thinking.

I need to ask God to change my rebellious heart and make me willing to "turn my will and my life over to the care of God" (Step Three). I need to ask God to make me *want* to submit my desires to His—in all areas of life. Until I can do that authentically, I have needed to take a step back and ask God to make me willing to yield my will to His.

And importantly, rather than asking God to give me more strength to resist my sinful desires (the things I really wish I could do), I acknowledge those desires while handing them over to God. My heart wants to be right with God.

RELEASING ATTACHMENTS TO HARMFUL THOUGHTS AND BEHAVIORS

Putting this desired change of heart into action, I have needed to begin the difficult work of releasing my harmful or unhealthy thoughts, beliefs, judgments, feelings, impulses, behaviors, habits, and relationships. Moving away from these things begins with releasing my *attachments* to them—meaning my dependence on them, my longing for them, my identifying with them, my sense of entitlement to hold onto them—and my reluctance to let them go.

In particular, I released my dependence on lust as a coping mechanism, distraction, or entertainment. This includes turning over to God my attachment to my "right" to lust, with all its justifications. No amount of religious practice, inner healing, or personal growth can bring real peace if I were to continue to use lust or act on other harmful sexual thoughts or behaviors. It's important to recognize that *acting* on my attractions is different from just *feeling* my attractions, which I have little to no control over.

I have needed to release my resentments and blame of anyone or anything that may have led me to experience incongruent same-sex attractions. Along the way, I have had to do the difficult spiritual work of accepting and forgiving—myself as well as others, such as my father and brother.

When I speak of surrendering resistance to change (or to healing or growth), I am not promoting the idea that one's sexual orientation or core arousal template is going to change or even *needs* to change. Mine hasn't. I do not believe in, nor do I support, any so-called conversion therapy that attempts to force a change in a person's sexual orientation or pressure someone into trying to change it. Nor do I believe that sexual orientation will change if one just prays hard enough. Like so many others, I have tried desperately to pray my SSA away, with no success.

However, I do recognize, and have seen for myself, that with God's help and by humbly submitting to His will, the frequency and intensity of lustful temptations can lessen significantly. Authentic surrender is not a painful, white-knuckled suppression of lustful desires. Rather, humbly and consciously turning our sins and temptations over to God ultimately will lead to a much more peaceful, much less conflicted life and, in fact, a life of joy. That is what has happened even when my core sexual orientation and arousal templates have not changed. After all, there is no sin in being tempted. Even Jesus experienced severe temptations. But He abstained from all sin.

That is what has worked for me: abstaining from activities that are outside my religious teachings while surrendering the idea that my core arousal template needs to change. As all of us do, I have chosen my sexual identity (how I "label" myself or the meaning I give to my particular sexual feelings and experiences). I chose my sexual expression (my behaviors and values). However, I did not choose my arousal template.

It's clear to me from years of clinical experience that same-sex attractions can develop differently in different people. I know men who have reported their lived experience as having always felt same-sex attracted, from their earliest memories. For these men, there was typically no abuse. It appears that when God "knits" us in our mother's womb (Psalms 139:13), He allows many of us to experience or be predisposed to certain challenges from birth. Could this not also sometimes be the case with our sexual natures?

I know other men who were sexually abused or groomed into same-sex experiences that altered their arousal template toward the same sex. I know still other men whose arousal template seems to have developed by unconsciously and unintentionally eroticizing their unmet needs or emotional wounds. This may develop, at least in some cases, in response to a strong yearning for a loving, engaged father figure or a need to feel included, welcomed, or safe among same-sex peers. Still, others may never be able to see how their arousal template developed to somehow include attraction to males. This may always remain a mystery to them.

Whatever the case, when it comes to the orientation of an arousal template (heterosexual, bisexual, or homosexual, among others), I have yet to meet someone who has completely reversed his attraction-orientation template from same-sex to opposite-sex. However, I do recognize that sexuality can sometimes be experienced as a moving pendulum where attractions can be influenced by life circumstances and relationships. My experience of the ebbs and flows of the intensity or intrusiveness of my attractions is sort of a barometer or indicator of how well I am getting my needs met for healthy self-care, healthy brotherly interactions, and a strong spiritual connection to God.

I have treated many individuals with pornography addictions who have reported a lifelong heterosexual orientation who, in search of ever-more titillating material, began to explore transexual or same-sex erotic material, which then altered (or broadened, rather) their heterosexual-attraction orientation. (Could this experience explain Romans chapter 1:24, "Therefore God gave them over in the lusts of their hearts to impurity, so that their bodies would be dishonored among them"?) But I've never met someone who had a homosexual or bisexual attraction orientation whose attractions shifted exclusively to heterosexual.

I don't believe that a sexual orientation change should ever be the real goal anyway. The goal for me was to be able to live at peace and in alignment with God's desires while becoming congruent within the community. This is where I have found true happiness and contentment: integrating my outward Christian heterosexual identity by allowing others to know my internal same-sex attraction incongruence while living in congruence with my testimony. Through faith in Christ, I have been released from the fear of other people's judgments of knowing my same-sex attraction. This alone has been a gift from God. It is no longer the silent, heavy burden I carried for 40 years of my life.

CHAPTER 8: THE ABSTINENCE PRINCIPLE

- - - - - - - - - - - - - - - - - - - -

"Abstain from Fleshly Lusts, Which Wage War Against the Soul"[11]

IN 2003, I BEGAN LOOKING AT WHAT WAS WRITTEN IN THE BIBLE. I was 32 years old and considered myself a Christian. I had just never studied the word of God. Curious, I began listening to a narration of the New Testament on tape in the morning when I would get ready for work. There were two words I heard that were recurring throughout the New Testament: "abstain" and "practice." Abstinence resonated with me as a recovering alcoholic. It is common to crave alcohol in early recovery. Yet I was advised to abstain as I worked through the Twelve Steps of the program.

The psychiatry profession's Diagnostic and Statistical Manual of Mental Health Disorders, DSM5, highlights the brain changes that occur during substance-use disorders ("A pathological pattern of use when exposed to drug-related stimuli," APA, 2014). The diagnosis of a substance-use disorder changes to early remission at three months of abstinence and sustained remission at one year of abstinence, largely attributed to the healing that occurs in the brain (APA, 2014).

Having abstained from alcohol since April 1, 2001, I still have cravings to get drunk every so often. Driving by a little sports bar on a Saturday afternoon every now and again I might think, "It would be wonderful to belly up to the bar and drink all day." I know the thought is ridiculous; it would be disastrous were I to begin drinking again. If I did return to alcohol consumption, I would quickly be drinking at the same levels or more than when I left off. With my organs decades older, and less capable of processing such toxins, I'd quickly find myself in trouble. Yet the thought is there, even while knowing it would be against my own well-being, my family's, and other drivers on the road, were I to drink again. When the thought does show up, I thank it for sharing and continue to abstain.

Similarly, I have determined that acting on same-sex attraction would be against my well-being. I have chosen to live a heterosexual life, but it does not mean the thoughts don't show up on occasion. God created us as sexual beings. Everyone has experienced unwanted sexual thoughts. I thought Jay Stringer's book *Unwanted* was brilliant in its messaging even before I read the first page.

1 Peter 2:11 challenges us, "Beloved, I urge you as aliens and strangers to abstain from fleshly lusts which wage war against the soul." Notice that the Holy Spirt chose the word abstain. The indication is that if we are acting on fleshly lusts that are not aligned with His intention for healthy relationships, it will bring discontent. Carnes (2006) notes in one of his meditations for individuals in recovery for sex addiction:

> After we act out, we usually say it was not worth it. It was either a disappointment, a catastrophe, or a near disaster. Even when acting out is at its "best" – we are filled with visions of what will happen if we are discovered. Or

we obsess with self-judgment and self-loathing. We calculate our losses in terms of time, money, and opportunity. We shudder at the risks we took. We live in fear of discovery, consequences, or even arrest.

Many today would tell someone with SSA who abstains from acting on those feelings that they are denying who they "really" are, and that the healthy course of action is to live openly as gay. Dr. Robert Weiss, author of the book "Cruise Control" notes in Chapter 4 that "the primary issue is not your attraction to men, even though this may feel like the problem, your biggest concern is the kind of clandestine sexual acting out that compels you to lie to loved ones putting them and yourself at risk. You have two choices, you may come out to yourself or others as an openly gay or bisexual man. Another option is to seek healthier ways to find or remain in a heterosexual partnership without self-hatred. There are supportive nonjudgmental therapies that can lead to a far healthier life than one of secrecy and the ongoing risk of public or private humiliation. However, by not finding a way to understand and accept your sexual attraction to men or by trying to become straight, you set yourself and others up for future pain and heartache." We believe the protocol outlined in this book is one such therapeutic approach.

I personally have great respect for those in the LGBTQ+ community. Everyone has the right to self-determination. Their struggles have been my struggles as we all strive to find our way in this world. I would be lying if I were to say I knew exactly why God views homosexuality outside of His design for healthy living. But for me, that does not matter. I believe God is real, and that He is the creator of this universe.

In Scripture, long before science could prove its accuracy, there are many passages that could only be scientifically verified within the last 300 years or so. I will not list them here, but Arnold Schnable, a former engineer at The Boeing Company, details them in his book *Has God Spoken?*

I had faith prior to reading his book. After reading it, I had evidence apart from my own experience. I desire to please God more than I desire to please man because I want to be in His kingdom when I depart from this world. In 1 Corinthians 6, the Holy Spirit lists what He finds to be sexually immoral—and practicing homosexuality is on the list. I didn't create the list, but I choose to respect it.

"Beloved, I urge you as aliens and strangers to abstain from fleshly lusts which wage war against the soul," Peter tells us in 1 Peter 2:11.

This chapter in 1 Peter offers insight into my relationship with Christ. Remember when I shared that my fantasies (sports, finances, achievement, sexual experiences) involve longing to be desired, affirmed, wanted, and accepted—or in short, loved? As we've "chatted over a cup of coffee" at various times, my sexual fantasies and arousal templates have shared with me where my wounds reside.

The verses leading up to 1 Peter 2:11 also indicate how they can heal because I have been chosen, desired, affirmed, wanted, and accepted by Christ. 1 Peter 2:1–10 states:

Therefore, [put] aside all malice and all deceit and hypocrisy and envy and all slander. Like newborn babies, long for the pure milk of the word so that by it you may grow in respect to salvation, if you have tasted the kindness of the Lord.

And coming to Him as to a living stone which has been rejected by men but is choice and precious in the sight of God, you also, as living stones, are being built up as a spiritual sacrifice acceptable to God through Jesus Christ. For this is contained in scripture:

"BEHOLD, I LAY IN ZION A CHOICE STONE, A PRECIOUS CORNER STONE, AND HE WHO BELIEVES IN HIM WILL NOT BE DISAPPOINTED." This precious value, then, is for you who believe; but for those who disbelieve, "THE STONE WHICH THE BUILDERS REJECTED, THIS BECAME THE VERY CORNER STONE," and, "A STONE OF STUMBLING AND ROCK OF OFFENSE"; for they stumble because they are disobedient to the word, and to this doom they were also appointed. But you are a chosen race, a royal priesthood, a holy nation, a people for God's own possession, so that you may proclaim the excellencies of Him who called you out of darkness into His marvelous light; for you once were NOT A PEOPLE, but now you are the PEOPLE OF GOD; you had NOT RECEIVED MERCY, but now you have RECEIVED MERCY.

In my early 20s, during my active alcohol addiction, I would sometimes "hook up" with a friend after a night of drinking. This went off and on for about a year. After each occasion, I felt a hole— or an emptiness—inside me. It never felt natural. Immediately after the sexual release, darkness settled in. The sexual attractions or temptations have never gone away completely, although they are much less intense and less frequent than they were in those days. I realize there is much I don't know about the spiritual realm, but I can sense when I am under attack. I press on, knowing that through continued abstinence, I am sanctified—made holy, freed, and purified. 1 Thessalonians 4:3–7 notes:

> For this is the will of God, your sanctification; that is, that you abstain from sexual immorality; that each of you know how to possess his own vessel in sanctification and honor, not in lustful passion, like the Gentiles who do not know God; and that no man transgress and defraud his brother in the matter because the Lord is the avenger in all these things, just as we also told you before and solemnly warned you. For God has not called us for the purpose of impurity, but in sanctification.

As I shared in chapter 5, I attended the Journey into Manhood intensive in 2022 alongside 25 other men from various faiths, ethnicities, and backgrounds who had experienced same-sex attraction throughout their lives. Journey into Manhood (JiM) is designed "especially for men to address internal conflicts over their sexual thoughts, feelings, identity, values, and behaviors—in a compassionate yet challenging environment of self-discovery, inner healing, radical acceptance, and brotherly support" (Brothers Road, 2022).

You'll recall that I shared that I have spoken with friends and clients about how their sense of acceptance might change if they felt known and accepted in their church communities. At the JiM weekend, I similarly spoke with several individuals with SSA who believed that their own feelings of being accepted by God, self, and others would dramatically increase if their faith communities knew about their SSA and viewed their choice of abstaining as honorable, were encouraging, and supported their walk with God.

These men experienced something similar to what Amnesty International had discovered—that victims of trauma only began to experience real self-acceptance and healing when they were able to connect with others who had survived a similar trauma. Likewise, at this weekend intensive, these SSA men experienced sharing their past traumas, fears, and shame in a like-minded community of men who came from similar backgrounds. As they felt seen and accepted just as they were, they experienced a level of healing and love that, sadly, many had never experienced from their faith communities.

I have found over the years that the wisdom of God shows up in many different places. For example, the Twelve Steps are not unique teachings. Each of the steps has a biblical basis. Likewise, each has a therapeutic basis as well. The Twelve Steps were developed, apparently, without consultation with biblical or therapeutic authority. But truth showed up anyway.

Similarly, the teachings I heard at the JiM weekend rang true because they shined a light on my pre-existing, or intuitive, beliefs and values as well as many therapeutic and biblical truths. The power of knowing other men who shared my burdens and goal of abstinence enabled me to do something I had never thought possible two short years ago: to tell my church family about my SSA.

At my congregation, the members take turns providing Sunday morning sermons; our preacher is more of an outreach minister. I really tend to like this as it gives the opportunity to hear from other members of the church. A few days prior to my scheduled Sunday sermon, I reviewed what I had prepared with my wife, Holly. After going through the entire lesson, I waited for her opinion.

"Well, what do you think?" I asked.

Holly's face was unimpressed. "I liked it, but I've heard it all before," was her candid reply.

"Yes, but it's the first time that I am directly stating that I struggle with same-sex attraction—versus talking about it only indirectly through Scripture."

Still no change in Holly's demeanor. "Oh, well yes, like I said I liked it."

I continued probing Holly for more input and what parts of the sermon she felt resonated with her the most. It was a pleasant conversation, but it was life changing. We were united, which was all that really mattered.

That Sunday, with my children in the audience, I revealed my testimony, which included my experience of abstaining from incongruent feelings of same-sex attraction. Midway through the sermon, I noticed my oldest daughter get up and leave. I had shared my lifelong struggles with my daughters earlier that year but wondered if my sharing it publicly had a negative impact. But driving home, I received a text message from my oldest daughter. It read, "Woo hoo! (emoji with face blowing on a party favor while wearing a party hat) Good job on the sermon. Sorry I had to leave early for work." My fears about why my daughter might have walked out during my sermon were completely unfounded. I had tears in my eyes while taking in my daughter's affirmation.

No one at church had a negative reaction. And why would they? I shared a burden of the flesh, my commitment through Christ, and a desire to abstain to be in alignment with God's word. While everyone's burden may be different, we all choose to abstain from something. My issue that morning just happened to be SSA. No better and no worse than anyone else.

CHAPTER 9: NEEDS FULFILLMENT

- -

"And My God Will Supply All Your Needs According to His Riches"[12]

FOR ME, THE MOST RELEVANT PRINCIPLE OF ABSTINENCE THROUGH Christ falls under a broad category of inner work that Brothers Road calls "Needs fulfillment."

It is never enough to simply abstain from sin or unhealthy behaviors. We have to replace those negative behaviors with positive ones. I think of it this way: It's impossible to make a river stop flowing. We can only redirect it. All that water needs someplace else to go.

Likewise, when we break old habits or withdraw from established addictions or simply abstain from acting on temptations, we have to do something else instead with our energy, thoughts, and behaviors. Something better. Something healing and healthy.

When we think of core emotional, social, and spiritual needs, we begin with the reality that a man needs to genuinely like, accept, and respect himself.

He needs to build a strong sense of self-worth. He needs to genuinely like who he is and who he is becoming. He needs courage and self-confidence to even embark on this journey that is, in so many ways, counter-cultural today. He needs inner healing from past hurts that otherwise may be blocking him from liking and accepting who he is. This requires the inner strength to recognize, feel, process, and reconcile his emotions—without harming others. He needs courage to be truthful and authentic with himself and others about who he really is.

The sad truth is that when we suppress and deny authentic needs like these, those unmet needs can demand to express themselves in any way possible—often in harmful ways, such as through unhealthy or sinful relationships, self-hate, shame, and destructive methods of self-comfort.

The second and third "core needs" that Brothers Road identifies are the needs for brotherhood and a tribe—a place of belonging. This is where the church could provide life-changing love, acceptance, discipleship, and support.

A man needs attention, acknowledgment, affection, and acceptance of who he really is, especially from other men and those he respects and values most. He needs male peers, mentors, father figures, and friends who uniquely challenge and affirm each other as only men can.

He needs a place where he knows he belongs and is wanted, included, valued, respected, and affirmed. He needs to be part of a tribe (community, family, brotherhood, group, or cause) that shares a common purpose, similar values, and who help lift each other up and make each other better. Ultimately, he needs to contribute at least as much to his tribe as he receives.

Men who suppress and deny needs like these can too easily latch on to anyone (even strangers online or anonymous hook-ups) who seem to offer acceptance—no matter how, or how fleeting, or at what price. Without a safe place where he knows he belongs and is accepted and wanted (*are you listening, church communities?*), a man is at risk of joining any group that will have him, no matter how unhealthy the group.

A fourth core need that Brothers Road identifies is a need to love and be loved. Love is the greatest human need. A broken man cannot authentically give love until he can first experience it and receive it. Suppressing this need doesn't make it go away. Rather, it can express itself in false or harmful imitations of love, such as toxic relationships, pornography, sexual hook-ups, or other destructive behaviors.

The last two core needs that I'll reference are what Brothers Road calls an anchor and a mission.

A man needs to find and hold onto the core beliefs and values that will anchor his life and keep him grounded and centered even when the world shifts around him. Many men find this in a personal relationship with God. From his core beliefs and values (as well as his sense of purpose and meaning), a man forms his self-identity—a definition and vision of himself that, consciously or unconsciously, will set the entire course of his life.

When he ignores this need for an anchor, a man can flounder, adrift, and become susceptible to latching onto whatever others tell him to believe or who they tell him he should be.

Likewise, a man needs a mission. He needs a higher purpose, meaningful work, or to serve a cause greater than himself. He needs his life to have meaning beyond serving himself and his own wants and needs. As he grows and heals from whatever emotional pain he has from his past, he naturally starts to shift his focus toward serving and giving. This usually means turning his heart to God and following where God's spirit leads him.

Without a mission and meaning, a man can become self-absorbed, less able to love, and stuck in past wounds and victimhood.

A Biblical Perspective (Scott)

Biblically speaking, each and every item on Brothers Road's needs wheel matches Scripture. The very definition of what it means to be human comes from God when He says in Genesis that we are "made in His image." God found it important to convey our worth to us so that we could understand that our lives have meaning and value. We aren't cosmic accidents; we are children of God, and John 3:16 tells us how much God values us. God loves us enough to send His son to die for us—that's real value!

Unfortunately, knowing that God loves me is not the same as me liking, accepting, and respecting myself. Paul struggled with looking at the man in the mirror. When we think of the things we have done wrong or the right things we have failed to do, it is very easy to lose respect for ourselves. Read Paul's description of himself in Romans 7, and it is likely you will feel the same frustration with your own behavior. So, what is the answer? Paul gives it when he says, "Wretched man that I am, who will deliver me from this body of death? Thanks be to God through Jesus Christ our Lord! So then, I myself serve the law of God with my mind, but with my flesh I serve the law of sin" (Romans 7:24–25).

When I know that Jesus died for me even when I was resisting His will, and that He understands that I am trying to serve Him—my need for respect and acceptance can be fulfilled.

The other items on the needs wheel are also seen throughout Scripture: The need for brothers? The Bible speaks openly about the benefit that was gained by David and Jonathan's relationship. Those two men loved each other as their own souls and their souls were knit together (1 Samuel 18:1). There was nothing sexual in the bond between David and Jonathan—it was two men who had a tight friendship, mutual respect for each other, and worked tirelessly together toward shared goals. They fought side by side and served as fellow soldiers and companions together over many years. Those sorts of bonds are immense blessings.

Proverbs speaks of the need for brotherhood when it says, "A man of many companions may come to ruin, but there is a friend who sticks closer than a brother" (Proverbs 18:24). You don't need a lot of friends to meet the need for brotherhood, but everyone needs quality bonds with people. Unfortunately, the world offers many of those bonds in the form of unhealthy relationships. The key is to meet those needs with authenticity and with alignment with spiritual values.

The same is true with the need for a tribe. The book of Hebrews warns Christians not to neglect assembling together because it is when the church is gathered together that we are best able to encourage one another, strengthen one another, and stir each other up to live as we ought. The church should be our tribe, not merely a Sunday morning spot in the pew.

The church is meant to be a family. If a brother is someone who is a lot like you and can bring you strength, a tribe is a group of people who bring you strength because they are diversely different from you. The church has from its inception been designed by God to be made up of people from vastly different backgrounds and personalities.

In chapter 12 of Paul's letter to the Corinthians, he describes the church as a body made up of various parts that is stronger because each brings different strengths while being guided by one Head, Jesus. We need that sort of diversity because where you are weak, another will be strong. And the opposite is also true: You will have moments to share your strength where others are weak. Every man needs that sort of tribe to fit within. Jesus intended for it to be His church.

We also need opportunities to love and be loved. In the book of Judges, Samson is a tragic figure. At every point we see him seeking love. It didn't matter that he was the strongest man alive. It didn't matter that he was practically invincible. Samson wanted love, and in the end, he allowed himself to be tricked by Delilah because he would rather be manipulated by an unhealthy relationship than have no relationship at all.

God designed humans for relationship and connection. The very first thing God ever said that was "not good" in this world was "it is not good for man to be alone" (Genesis 2:18).

We also need an anchor. God speaks about many things being involved in the salvation process, from Jesus to faith to baptism to confession ... but one of the least talked about item on that list is "hope." Romans 8:24 literally says, "For in this hope we were saved." Hope is a requirement to live a life of faith in Jesus because hope anchors us.

Hebrews 6:19 says, "We have this hope as a sure and steadfast anchor of the soul." Hope is a need because it is the thing that keeps us from becoming despondent and drifting when the waves of life get high and dangerous. A man without hope will often run straight toward sexual temptation because if he has no hope, he will lose his will to fight.

If you have SSA, there is hope. You can live a profoundly blessed and fulfilling Christian life. You can serve the Lord and abstain from sexual temptation. You can be victorious.

So often, when I meet men struggling with pornography or other sexual sins, they have given up hope. They have struggled for so long (often since their pre-teen years) that they have lost their hope of ever overcoming and living without this hidden shame. No man will be strong and victorious without hope. We must instill it in one another.

Men are also meant to live physical lives. God created Adam to work. Work existed in the Garden of Eden. The curse of sin introduced the difficulties of work, but work in and of itself is a righteous endeavor. We are meant to toil with our hands and change the world by carving it according to our imaginations.

Just look at modern suburbia—lawns as far as the eye can see. We landscape our yards with rocks dug from quarries, plants imported from climates half a world away, and grass cultivated for the peculiar purpose of only growing two to three inches before being mown down again. From landscaping to skyscrapers to great machinery like the automobile and the airplane—we can't help ourselves. As humans, we build, we work, we shape, and we find purpose in our labor.

Having said that, we also live in a time where many men are able to work without being physical. Desk jobs, white collar work, and remote office Zoom meetings have led to a culture where it is possible to never leave your home and engage your body in any physicality. I know many men that have never had callused hands or known the blessing of fatigue that comes from a hard day of physical labor.

Many of our modern first-world problems such as sleep disorders, depression, and anxiety may be greatly improved, and in some cases entirely alleviated, by physical activity. In a modern era where physical activity is not required, it is becoming clear that it is more of a necessity than ever.

And part of that is because the next need on the wheel is also true—men need to be challenged. We need to be challenged physically, but even more so, we need to be challenged spiritually.

The language of competition is throughout the New Testament. In 1 Corinthians 9, Paul compares the life of a Christian to a boxing match and a marathon, and he compares Christians to athletes needing to discipline their bodies, endure self-imposed hardship, and exercise self-control in order to win a prize. Paul even warned the Christians that it is "through many tribulations we must enter the kingdom of God" (Acts 14:22).

Though we often hate the pain that comes with being challenged, the challenge is what makes us get up in the morning. We are meant to do hard things. Throughout the book of Proverbs, the Holy Spirit tells us not to be lazy, to rise early, and to not procrastinate. Ecclesiastes 9:10 says it plainly, "Whatever your hand finds to do, do it with your might, for there is no work or thought or knowledge or wisdom in Sheol [i.e., the grave] to which you are going."

Furthermore, we see this in how God interacts with us. Our Heavenly Father is constantly disciplining and pushing His children to bring the best out of them. Hebrews 12:6 says, "For the Lord disciplines the one He loves, and chastises every son whom He receives." God challenges us and disciplines us because He loves us. Challenges reveal our weaknesses so that we can learn from them, give us a sense of accomplishment and worth, and prepare us to not be quitters. A man that can learn to overcome challenges in one area can learn to overcome them in other areas. Men need a challenge to be men.

And the last item on the needs wheel is a "mission." We are told to imitate Jesus. Jesus lived with purpose. In His darkest hour, as He prepared to face the excruciating pain of the cross, Jesus said, "Now is my soul troubled. And what shall I say? 'Father, save me from this hour'? But for this purpose, I have come to this hour." (John 12:27). Do you notice what kept Jesus going? He knew His purpose, and by having a mission, He was able to face the darkness.

Men without a mission act like children. Men with a mission can face horrible things and stare down impossible circumstances with valor and honor. The German philosopher Frederich Nietzsche once said, "He who has a *Why*, can bear any *How*." I believe he was correct. In his exceptional biography, Victor Frankl describes what helped him and other Jewish captives endure the atrocities of the Holocaust. The name of the book tells you everything you need to know: <u>Man's Search for Meaning</u>. Men must find their why.

One of the greatest deceptions perpetrated by today's hypersexualized culture is that your sexual desires are supposed to be your why—but that's a horrible lie and egregiously damaging to the generations that are being taught it. Sex and desire are parts of life, but they are not the meaning of life. We are not animals to simply be driven by our passions and lusts. God made you in His image and we ought to set our minds above. The Scriptures give us the mission we are made for—and the mission men need.

CHAPTER 10: TOGETHER IN LOVE

"Naked and Not Ashamed"

A FEW MONTHS AFTER ATTENDING THE JOURNEY INTO MANHOOD weekend, Holly and I made our way down to Tennessee in January 2023 to attend the Together in Love couples weekend retreat. The retreat is intended for couples dealing with the challenges of SSA who are committed to their marriages and the healing journey. The weekend provides a safe, caring environment for you to meet other couples who want more for their marriage, to spend focused time learning to communicate skillfully, play intentionally, and grow deliberately as a couple (https://www.illuminatethepath. com/retreat-together-in-love-1, 2022).

On the drive, Holly suggested, "I don't really see why we're going to this retreat because your SSA doesn't affect our marriage, unless there is something you're not telling me."

I understood what Holly was saying. We hardly fight, we're on the same page with parenting, we have a healthy sexual relationship, and we are faithful to each other. However, I wanted to share our journey as a committed, loving couple in a mixed-orientation marriage. I also wanted to publish the FB-AACP Therapy protocol, and I had a tremendous of fear integrating my SSA into my professional and spiritual worlds. I felt that we (more so, I) needed to meet other couples who had similar lived experiences to help further validate my own experience and help me build the confidence and courage to become increasingly public in sharing my story and counseling others.

When we arrived, we didn't know what to expect. After checking into our room, we made our way to the main hall where chairs were formed in a large circle. Holly and I chatted with a few couples prior to making our way to our seats. Looking around, we saw couples with faces you could encounter anywhere. Our hosts, Darryl and his wife, Terry, kicked off the event with introductions. Another married couple and a widowed man, Bobby, helped facilitate the event. Bobby was a man in his mid-70s whose lifelong spouse had passed away from cancer two-and-a-half years earlier. But she was there in spirit throughout the weekend as he shared glimpses into their journey, love, and commitment to each other. I thought this was a beautiful reminder of the cycles of life in that the love for a dear spouse continues even when our bodies depart this world.

The weekend may have been typical of any couples retreat with respect to content. We had exercises on reflective listening, written self-clearings, healing dialogues, along with several experiential processes. Most memorable for me was an experiential process involving finger-painting on canvas. Blindfolded, couples were tasked with creating a painting that was reflective of their relationship over the years. It began with each partner blindly choosing two colors each (among eight), then, still blindfolded, jointly finger-painted our feelings about our marriage.

When we were able to view the results of our "artwork," part of Holly's contributions included dark purple blotches during the first round, which to me was surprising. She later shared that these represented her internal battles with food and a lifelong struggle with an eating disorder. I was aware of Holly's eating disorder throughout our marriage, but this exercise revealed that she carried this battle with the same emotion in which I carried my SSA ... with a deep sense of shame.

Next, couples were tasked with painting their feelings and perspectives of the future of their marriage. While Holly and I had chosen different colors the first time we had been blindfolded, when blindfolded again for the second part of the assignment, by chance (or perhaps by divine providence), we both chose the same colors, blue and green.

We were able to remove the blindfolds for this next part of the assignment, reflecting on our future together. I created a waterfall out of her dark emotions that fed a stream flowing with life. When it was Holly's turn, she also painted springs of water and greenery. When we came together for the reveal, Holly, and I chose to write a Bible verse at the top of our painting: 2 Cor 12:9–10, which says:

> "My grace is sufficient for you, for power is perfected in weakness. Most gladly, therefore, I will rather boast about my weaknesses, so that the power of Christ may dwell in me. Therefore, I am well content with weaknesses, with insults, with distresses, with persecutions, with difficulties, for Christ's sake; for when I am weak, then I am strong."

Holly and I had become figuratively "naked" in our authenticity and vulnerability with each other. And yet we were unashamed

(Genesis 2:25). Our separate brokenness, so intimately seen by each other, had been made whole through the love of Christ who brought us together.

Below is a picture of our painting which hangs on the wall in our bedroom.

With gratitude but also deep compassion, Holly and I humbly recognize how the effects of my SSA journey have been much less threatening to our relationship as a couple than is often true with many other marriages, especially where there have been years of hiding and deceit or even serial same-sex adultery. In cases like that, the traumatic impact on the betrayed spouse can hardly be overstated.

In such cases, I strongly encourage individual and couples counseling with professionals who are well-trained in the effects of betrayal trauma on relationships. It's true that many marriages collapse due to betrayal and loss. But it is also true that many marriages survive and repair what they once thought could never be repaired. I've seen couples become even closer than they were before, with more honesty and true partnership than they had had originally. Forgiveness, love, and restoration of trust will likely be a long, difficult, and emotionally taxing process with many ups and downs, with forward leaps followed by discouraging setbacks.

But through the grace of God, restoration is real. Sanctification is real. Not just for individuals but for couples, too. If it is God's will, and if both husband and wife are willing to do meaningful emotional and spiritual healing work, you can emerge stronger—and more connected—than ever before.

I have included a list of suggested resources for couples working through betrayal trauma in the appendix.

CHAPTER 11: AUTHENTICITY AND THE CONGRUENCY PRINCIPLE:

"Do Not Be Like the Hypocrites"[13]

"Many also of those who had believed kept coming, confessing and disclosing their practices," Luke tells us in Acts 19:18.

AS THE NAME OF THE LORD JESUS WAS BEING MAGNIFIED, THE FOL-lowers of "the Way" (as Luke often terms discipleship in the Book of Acts) in the first-century church were forming bonds, worshiping in each other's homes, and confessing and disclosing their practices (or in other words, their sins) (Acts 19:18). What a powerful image of healing community.

As noted in the previous chapter, 2 Corinthians 12: 9–10 states, "And He has said to me, 'My grace is sufficient for you, for power is perfected in weakness.' Most gladly, therefore, I will rather boast about my weaknesses, so that the power of Christ may dwell in me. Therefore, I am well content with weaknesses, with insults, with distresses, with persecutions, with difficulties, for Christ's sake; for when I am weak, then I am strong."

Throughout Scripture, God loves to use our weaknesses as a demonstration of His strength. The message is that the more we rely on His strength, the stronger we become—so strong and so authentic that we can begin boasting about our weaknesses, because we are relying on Him, not ourselves.

At the Journey into Manhood intensive, we learned that we had to "get real to heal." Isn't that something? Real. (I heard a man at a seminar once state, "What we often think looks bad to others may actually look good." He was talking about authenticity, allowing ourselves to be truly seen.) We were encouraged to stop hiding from ourselves and others and instead build trusted communities where we can be truly seen and known. We feel our feelings, and underneath all the shame and resistance, we uncover our authentic core emotions.

Like most boys who grow up to experience same-sex attractions, I spent much of my life hiding behind a mask, presenting a false version of myself that I thought others would accept. I am hardly alone. Many people with similar life experiences hide their true selves from others, afraid to let their authentic selves be seen or known. In fact, same-sex attracted individuals may have learned from their surroundings that emotions themselves are bad—especially anger, tears, and fear, especially for boys. Boys aren't supposed to feel their feelings. Boys are supposed to be strong, no matter what. They are often taught to hide and bury their emotions.

Often, boys who would later grow up to feel attracted to other males may have been born with personalities that are naturally more sensitive. This can be wonderful! This may make them more creative, artistic, empathic, and relational. But it can also be painful. They may be more emotionally volatile and more easily hurt. They may sense rejection where perhaps none is intended. They may tell themselves they don't fit in with other boys and give up trying. Too often, they may be bullied. They crave friendship and acceptance—but don't feel worthy of them.

One common way that these boys learn to keep their emotions hidden is to cope by escaping into fantasy, where they are always included, always wanted, always heroic. Some fantasies inadvertently turn sexual, giving those fantasies even more power and making them more seductive. But they can come at a very high price. More secrets to carry. More shame. They convince themselves they would be rejected if others found out about their shameful, secret thoughts.

So, they learn to wear masks. They smile and lie that everything is fine. It's not unusual for them sometimes to become over-achievers in an attempt to prove their worth to themselves and others. But inside, like me at one time, they may feel like they are silently dying.

I eventually discovered that the only way *out* of this pattern was *through*. I came to realize that I could never find real peace if I didn't open up to at least a few trusted confidants and reveal the hidden conflict inside of me.

My journey of authenticity about my sexuality began in 2005 when I was dating Holly, and I shared with her aspects of my sexual history and sexual shame. Instead of her rejecting me for it, my authenticity and vulnerability and her compassion and acceptance drew us closer together.

But not until 2021 did I make the decision to begin the journey of *full* congruency. I wasn't sure what this was going to look like, but I was being drawn to envision a life without hiding. When I had originally sought spiritual counseling from my friend Scott after my deployment, you may recall I initially had no intention of sharing the whole truth with him. As accepting, affirming, and helpful as Scott was, I wasn't sure what his reaction would be if I shared with him my lived experience of same-sex attraction. Scott and I had kept in touch throughout the years. Whenever I had a biblical question or needed insight into a spiritual matter, I'd reach out to him. Now, I needed a spiritual advisor who knew my whole story, so I reconnected with Scott once again.

We connected via a video call on a weekday. I had shared with Scott that I was on a professional journey of congruency and desired his feedback. I finally recounted what had taken place at my friend's house as a child, the attempted suicide, and the details of my same-sex attraction. Scott listened attentively and unflinchingly. We hadn't yet developed the FB-AACP principles, but I was verbalizing them as how I had chosen to live out my faith. Scott thanked me for reaching out and sharing this part of my life with him. We agreed to begin connecting once a week as I began to work out the vision of being congruent.

Because of the emotional risk I took to share my secrets with Scott, he was able to accept and love me as a brother in Christ for who I truly was, not some sanitized version of myself that I chose to represent to him. Apart from my spouse, Scott was my first authentic friend who knew my whole story. That was such a gift that he gave me, which I appreciated beyond measure.

Scott reflected on the teachings of Jesus who sees the real you and me and loves us right where we are at on the journey of life.

God calls for the exact same thing from His church.

This combination of experiences with revealing my secrets was the beginning of the end of nearly 40 years of shame. Shame is an especially debilitating emotion that keeps us trapped in self-hate and *anticipatory* rejection (we *expect* to be rejected even when we haven't been yet). It prevents us from feeling almost anything else. But when we "get real" with a few trusted others who respond with acceptance and compassion, our shame begins to collapse.

Those first disclosures felt like a huge risk. But once I felt authentically accepted by Holly and then by Scott, my shame began to shrink, and I began to believe that maybe others, as well, could love and accept me as I was

When I arrived at the Journey into Manhood intensive in Indiana, just the fact that I was there effectively "outed" me to the other participants, most of whom were there for the same reasons. It was a remarkable breath of fresh air to show up and be seen for who I was.

Accepting the challenge of being authentically known, when I returned from my Journey into Manhood experience, I reached out to schedule a meeting with my church elders. The elders were familiar with me as a fellow Christian, a licensed therapist, and someone in recovery from a substance-use disorder. However, they were unaware that my life journey also encompassed my long-standing history of same-sex attractions that I kept hidden. The elders showed no hesitation when I shared this aspect of my journey. It seemed to have no impact on their perception of me as a Christian brother in Christ.

The impact of this meeting on my spiritual and mental well-being is beyond measure. As I drove away from the church, I felt accepted, empowered, and sheltered under the church's authority. I felt truly understood. This marked a pivotal step in a year-long journey toward alignment with my family, congregation, and profession. Had the meeting with the elders been met with judgment or rejection, it may have kept me in silent shame for many more years.

The elders asked if I would be willing to give a sermon shortly thereafter, which was an honor. I gave two sermons over the course of a few months where I touched on my lived experience. With Holly and my children in the audience, I unfolded my childhood trauma, same-sex attraction, and the FB-AACP healing path. I was met with nothing but love. No one fell out of their pew. No harsh words. Just love.

Integrating my lived experience into my professional world was by far the scariest. I had several consultations with my business attorney, who is absolutely wonderful. I developed a reaction letter for clients who might potentially react negatively about learning their therapist had the lived experience of same-sex attraction but chose a life of abstaining from acting on those feelings to remain true to his faith. I met with each member of my team sharing my story and plans to go public. My entire staff encouraged me, affirming they were behind me 100%. I edited my practice biography to include my work on the website that Scott and I had created to support other Christians with same-sex attractions (biblicalsexualintegrity.org).

I held my breath and hit publish. It was out there on my practice website, for all to see.

The first no-show created panic in me. I reached out to Keith, one of my Christian brothers whom I met in Brothers Road. "I just lost my first client," I exclaimed, "after posting my bio." His words were reassuring, as if we were on the battlefield together. He reminded me to breathe. It was what I needed to hear. I reached back out to him later in the day when I learned the client had a work-related conflict; nothing to do with my bio. The journey of becoming congruent has gone from terrifying to freeing and beautiful.

The French philosopher Michel de Montaigne is credited with having once said about the irony of worry, "My life has been full of terrible misfortunes, most of which never happened." I often think of the boy staring in the mirror with the pamphlet of Jesus in his hand. So suicidal, so scared. I love him so much for hanging in there. I no longer have to hide or feel ashamed.

Authenticity isn't exclusively about disclosure and transparency. It's also a willingness to face and feel our authentic feelings rather than burying them and pretending they don't matter or don't exist. The saying goes, "You gotta feel it to heal it," and I really believe that's true.

Buried under shame are core emotions of fear, anger, and sadness. As debilitating as shame can be, no one likes to feel extreme fear, anger, or sadness, either. But while shame keeps us stuck, as if in emotional quicksand, core emotions like anger and sadness are typically transitory when we allow ourselves to feel them fully.

Think about it: Have you ever allowed yourself to have a really good cry and then felt calmer and more at peace afterward, even when nothing that caused your sadness had changed? That is the healing nature of allowing ourselves to fully feel and safely express our God-given emotions.

How unfortunate, then, that so many of us in the church learn to minimize, bury, and dismiss our legitimate sadness, anger, and fear. We may deny those feelings altogether ("Of course I'm not angry, I'm a Christian!") or rush to solutions like instant but contrived forgiveness.

Years ago, a pastor was interviewed on TV immediately after a school shooting left 15 people dead. He said, "We have to forgive those boys (the shooters)." Really? Sure, eventually, but not today! Today we mourn. Today we rage at the unfairness. Today we comfort each other. Forgiveness can't possibly be sincere if we dismiss the horrific wrong as insignificant without allowing ourselves to feel the injustice and grief.

But again, our true feelings can hurt. Why do you think there is so much alcoholism, pornography use, overeating, and endless online gaming, if not to avoid feeling our feelings? We often try to numb our feelings with these and other defenses and distractions.

Again, you gotta feel it to heal it. Even if we trick our minds, our hearts know when we are lying to ourselves about what we are really feeling.

Another common saying is that *time heals all wounds.* It's a reassuring thought, but it's rarely true. Have you ever had an obvious overreaction to a perceived slight? Any time your reaction seems out of proportion to an event, it's very likely that you are reacting not just to that event but to all the other times in life that you experienced something similar and never fully felt and released it. New hurts attach themselves to old, unhealed wounds. Buried pain festers and rots and finds sneaky ways to express itself indirectly—often by lashing out. Or acting out.

While authenticity almost certainly will require us to feel unhealed pain around old, unresolved issues, joy lies just on the other side.

For me, allowing myself to be truly seen and known, and discovering I can be loved and accepted anyway, relieved a lifelong burden of fear, shame, and isolation. Allowing myself to feeling underlying, unresolved emotions around past hurts freed me to live joyfully in the present as never before.

And this allows me to be in a loving, trusting relationship with God in a way I never could be if I were still hiding huge parts of myself from myself and others. I truly believe that living authentically makes me a much greater, more credible, more effective witness and servant of God.

A favorite song helps me anchor the truth that "the God of glory has made me a living, breathing testimony." It's called "Miracle Child," by Brandon Lake.

> I shouldn't be alive
> My future was six feet under
> One foot in the grave
> No hope to be saved
> I shouldn't be alive

But I'm a miracle child
Defied every diagnosis
And as close as it came
I can stand here and say
I'm a miracle child
Death, where is your sting?
My Savior's word is final
I am resurrected
Blood-protected
I am a miracle child
If you're facing the odds
If you think you're beyond His saving
There's no life He can't raise
No, your wounds aren't too great
He's a miracle God
'Cause He shouldn't be alive
His body was six feet under
Three days in the grave
But that stone rolled away
Yeah, our God is alive, oh
Death, where is your sting?
My Savior's word is final
I am resurrected
Blood-protected
I am a miracle child
You're the living, breathing God of glory
I'm a living, breathing testimony
You're the one who turns a dead-end story
To a living, breathing testimony
I'm a miracle child.

- -

A Further Biblical Perspective (Scott)

In the book of Matthew, chapter 23 stands out as different than all other chapters before or after. Matthew 23 is sometimes referred to as the "chapter of the seven woes" and it is the most visceral denunciation Jesus ever gives of His adversaries, the scribes, and Pharisees. For Jesus, this is the speech that most openly places Him in opposition to the religious elite of the day. He condemns their treatment of the poor, their judgmental attitudes, their love of fame and notoriety, but above all else, Jesus rebukes them for their hypocrisy.

Hypocrisy is another word for inauthenticity. A hypocrite is a pretender. Jesus compares them to a tomb that is washed and cleaned on the outside, but full of death inside. We often think of hypocrites as being malicious in their pretending, but that isn't always the case. Some hypocrites are simply trying to live a double life so that they don't need to face the realities of their struggles. The alcoholic may mask an addiction by being a "functional" alcoholic. The shopaholic hides from an ever-mounting burden of debt by wearing clothes, driving cars, and eating meals that make him feel rich even though the bank account says otherwise. Sometimes, the most depressed individuals hide their sorrow behind a masked smile. Whether through malicious intent or as a coping mechanism, the result is still the same—inauthentic living is hiding the truth from others, from God, and maybe even from yourself.

The scribes and Pharisees acted like they had no problems, so they didn't have to reveal the truth about their need for a savior. There are three major problems with this approach to living.

The first problem is that it hides from life instead of living it. The problems don't go away just because we put on a happy face. The alcohol is still a temptation, the bank account is still overdrawn, and the trauma is still untreated. Those struggling with same-sex attractions cannot address them until they are willing to admit them to themselves and others. It is inauthentic to bottle up our trials, trauma, and real life in such a way that we wall ourselves off from others. It is living a lie.

The apostle John says it this way, "If we say we have no sin, we deceive ourselves, and the truth is not in us. If we confess our sins, He is faithful and just to forgive us our sins and to cleanse us from all unrighteousness. If we say we have not sinned, we make Him a liar, and His word is not in us." (1 John 1:8–10).

If we pretend that we don't have struggles, we are playing a game of deception with the world around us that places a barrier between us and God, as well as us and those who might help. And it sets us up for failure. Peter tells us that "whatever overcomes a person, to that he is enslaved" (2 Peter 2:19). If someone is unable to genuinely own his struggles as well as his successes, then he has been enslaved by his need for a persona. Do not allow your need to impress others to become the idol that enslaves you. You will never be truly free until you can live authentically and be real about your strengths and your weaknesses.

The second problem is that even if you can hide from others, you can't hide from yourself. It is possible to fool your neighbors, your friends, your spouse, and the church, but you can't fool yourself. The individual with same-sex attractions knows he has them and must live with that struggle even if he manages to hide it from everyone else. Which means he probably spends every day feeling fake. Life as an impersonator is hard. It is hard emotionally, it is hard spiritually, and it is extremely stressful. Incongruent lives are hard to maintain. Eventually, in my experience, someone who doesn't address and integrate his past struggles in a way that enables him to talk openly about it with some sort of support group is likely to relapse into behavior he has been attempting to abstain from. Eventually, the hypocrisy catches up to the individual and he can't take the strain of maintaining a double life anymore.

The third problem is that inauthentic lives send the wrong message to those around you who may also be struggling. One of the most encouraging elements of Scripture are the examples of flawed individuals that God used, transformed, and redeemed. We feel drawn to the apostle Peter because we know of his foolishness, his denials of Christ, and his tendencies toward leaping before looking. The apostle Paul looms larger than life as an unattainable example of bravery and faith ... until you remember that he originally persecuted Christians and was in his own words, "as one untimely born." Paul did amazing things as an evangelist, but he also showed up late to the party because of his stubbornness. It is the blemishes and the defects in Peter and Paul's character that endear them to us. Their shortcomings remind us that we can succeed, too.

That is exactly what the apostle Paul meant when he said, "The saying is trustworthy and deserving of full acceptance, that Christ Jesus came into the world to save sinners, of whom I am the foremost. But I received mercy for this reason, that in me, as the foremost, Jesus Christ might display his perfect patience as an example to those who were to believe in him for eternal life" (1 Timothy 1:15–16).

If someone who has struggled with same-sex attractions is not open about that struggle and God's ability to redeem and help him navigate those desires, then he is denying the glory God justly deserves, and they prevent using their example as an opportunity to encourage the next individual who needs that support. Hiding our pasts and living incongruently damages you, but it also damages the people you might be able to help. If everyone's struggles are experienced in silos, there is no community, no encouragement, no stirring up of one another to love and good works. Inauthenticity breeds isolation, which is bad for you and bad for others, too. The hypocrite can neither help nor be helped.

Instead, God calls us to live real lives. Lives where we own our past, own our trauma, and own our sins. We can speak openly of mistakes without glorifying them. We should be willing to risk the feeling of shame to walk in the light and bask in the truth. Authenticity and congruency are hard, but worth it. Every great Bible hero has a story of redemption—living your redemptive story glorifies God.

CHAPTER 12: MASCULINITY AND PRACTICING RIGHTEOUS LIVING:

"Be on the Alert, Stand Firm in the Faith, Act Like Men, Be Strong"[14]

JOHN 3:21 NOTES, "BUT HE WHO PRACTICES THE TRUTH COMES TO the Light, so that his deeds may be manifested as having been wrought in God."

1 John 3:7–8 states, "Little children, make sure no one deceives you; the one who practices righteousness is righteous, just as He is righteous; the one who practices sin is of the devil; for the devil has sinned from the beginning."

Throughout the New Testament, God chooses to make the distinction between those who practice sin and those who practice righteousness. Note that God did not use the word "perfect" righteousness. The definition of "practice" is to "perform (an activity) or exercise (a skill) repeatedly or regularly in order to improve or maintain one's proficiency." We can practice getting better in our sin by throwing away all guardrails and pretenses, or we can practice getting better at righteousness. This does not mean we will not struggle, but we can practice right living.

The necessary emotional work to my healing from my childhood wounds, decades of hiding in the shadows, and the places my addictions took me when I was practicing sin will take a lifetime.

After presenting at Florida College, a Christian university, in 2023 (see chapter 5), the elders of my local congregation gave me the green light to facilitate a Seven Pillars of Freedom weekly workshop for our local church. Seven Pillars of Freedom is a program to help men in their pursuit of sexual integrity. Every Monday evening, I meet with Christian brothers who desire to practice right living. The internal battles are different for each brother who attends the group. However, we learn so much from each other's struggles. The program really is about gaining and improving upon the necessary life skills to be better Christian men. We practice and celebrate our masculinity on the battlefield of life.

1 Corinthians 16:13–14 cautions, "Be on the alert, stand firm in the faith, act like men, be strong. Let all that you do be done in love." This is biblical masculinity. 1 Peter 5:8 advises, "Be of sober spirit, be on the alert. Your adversary, the devil, prowls around like a roaring lion, seeking someone to devour." For men, practicing righteousness _is_ practicing masculinity.

While I firmly believe that the principles in this chapter on masculinity and righteous living are true for all men everywhere, they are especially vital for boys and men who experience same-sex attractions.

These men will often tell you that they grew up feeling detached from a genuine sense of their own masculinity. They just didn't feel "man enough" inside. They often felt alienated from their male peers, fathers, or even the male world generally. They struggled with feeling accepted, wanted, or like they belonged as "one of the guys." They often experienced conflicted and sometimes emasculating relationships with girls or women. Sometimes, they felt controlled or smothered by them. At other times, they were overly attached to or enmeshed with the feminine, making it all the more difficult to claim and own their own masculinity.

Christian author and psychologist James Dobson writes in his book *Bringing Up Boys*:

> Mothers make boys. Fathers make men. In infancy, both boys and girls are emotionally attached to the mother. In psychoanalytic language, Mother is the first love object. She meets all her child's primary needs.

> Girls can continue to grow in their identification with their mothers. On the other hand, a boy has an additional developmental task—to disidentify from his mother and identify with his father. At this point [beginning about eighteen months], a little boy will not only begin to observe the difference, he must now decide, "Which one am I going to be?" In making this shift in identity, the little boy begins to take his father as a model of masculinity. At this early stage, generally before the age of three, Ralph Greenson observed, the boy decides that he would like to grow up like his father.[160] This is a choice. Implicit in that choice is the decision that he would not like to grow up like his mother. According to Robert Stoller, "The first order of business in being a man is, 'don't be a woman.'"[15]

Same-sex-attracted boys and men usually need to work more consciously and deliberately than other males to develop their internal sense of masculinity and sense of naturally belonging to the tribe of men. To do this, they need to challenge unhealthy thinking and harmful beliefs about themselves and their maleness. This requires men and boys to surrender an idealized and unrealistic sense of who or what a "real man" needs to be. Comparing themselves to idealized, movie-idol, or sports-idol maleness makes it impossible to ever measure up.

I tell clients to stop focusing on the perceived differences between themselves and other men and focus instead on the many similarities. I encourage them to "own" their own masculinity—or their personal version of it, at least—as more than sufficient and equal to any other man's masculinity.

SSA boys and men need to actively and consciously work to develop their masculine traits, like assertiveness, independence, initiative, decisiveness, healthy risk-taking, standing up for themselves, and setting clear, appropriate boundaries with others.

These boys and men need to challenge themselves by taking the emotional and physical risks to participate in activities or experiences that they find "masculinizing"— meaning those things help connect them to a greater sense of their own masculinity— as well as activities that include them in the company of other men. I'm not necessarily talking about stereotypically masculine activities like football or working out at the gym (although they could be). I'm talking about activities that engage a man's sense of creativity, courage, risk-taking, productivity, and competence, among others.

Along with building a strong internal sense of masculinity—feeling intrinsically grounded in the masculine—a man needs to take the risk of including himself in the broader world of men in meaningful ways. This often involves doing the inner-healing work necessary to address same-sex emotional wounds (usually going back to childhood or youth) that may be blocking him from trusting and relating to men.

Men who are looking to find their place in the masculine world can find ways to relate to men as peers—neither better than nor less than themselves—by finding at least a few common interests, activities, or shared goals. They need to find or build meaningful male communities for themselves—without passively waiting for someone to invite them in. All men need a "tribe," or a place where we belong and know unquestioningly that we are welcome and wanted, especially a place where we can work together toward shared goals (see chapter 9).

Men who choose to do this healing work take the initiative to build strong, trusting personal bonds with other men. SSA men typically start out longing for a special "bromance" with one single best friend, sometimes even pointing to the friendship of David and Jonathan as their desired model (2 Samuel 1:26). But what men really need are the blessings of multiple, meaningful, platonic friendships with men who support, stretch, challenge, and affirm him. I suggest men look to Jesus as an example, with the 12 and other disciples who walked with him, learned from him, and provided much-needed companionship on his lonely, arduous mortal ministry.

In pursuing this critical developmental task of disidentifying from mother (or women) and identifying with father (or men) (see

Dobson), men often find it beneficial to establish meaningful mentoring relationships with men who have qualities that they admire and who take a personal interest in their growth. All men need father figures, mentors, coaches, and elders throughout their lives.

By taking steps like these, men prove to themselves and others that they do, in fact, belong in the world of men. This is something men must claim; it cannot be given to us.

Our inborn drive to claim our masculinity is not exclusively about our internal sense of manhood and our interpersonal sense of belonging in the masculine world. Perhaps most importantly, it is about developing a healthy relationship with women and the feminine world as equal but, "other," and our God-given role as providers and protectors of families and communities.

Just as men must consciously earn and claim their sense of the masculine, they must consciously work to develop healthier relationships with women. A good place to begin is by challenging any unhealthy thinking and harmful beliefs about women. This often requires exploring possible inner-healing work around any opposite-sex wounding that may have kept a man stuck in negative attitudes. This usually includes exploring and challenging any transference of unhealthy relationships with women in their past (mothers? sisters? peers? teachers?) onto women in the present.

Unhealed wounds and unmet needs can teach a man a lot about himself and where his inner-healing work lies. Revisiting those old wounds can be painful. It may require grief work to release their negative hold on the man's life today. The purpose is not to blame or to justify his own destructive attitudes and behaviors toward women. The purpose is to become free from defining women by the harmful experiences of his past. It is to come to respect women as daughters of God who have their own strengths and weaknesses, their unhealed wounds, and unmet needs, and who are on their own healing journeys.

The goal is for a man to be firmly grounded in his masculinity, compassionate and strong, unyielding in practicing righteousness in all his relationships and interactions with women.

"Be on the alert, stand firm in the faith, act like men. Let all that you do be done in love" (1 Corinthians 6:13–14).

Fortunately for me, the women in my life have truly been a blessing. My mother did her best to raise four children on her own. She worked full-time, cooked, cleaned, and always made me feel loved and affirmed. I have fond memories of her bringing home McDonald's for dinner on a Friday evening. Eating two hamburgers and a small fry while watching *Dukes of Hazard* is a memory that comforts my soul. I still have an emotional connection to the comfort food of McDonald's, which is linked to my mother's love. She is the one who became my advocate when I was suicidal and refusing to return to school. Similarly, Holly has always made me feel loved and affirmed.

Looking back on the horizon of my life, the women (sisters, peers, and teachers) have been truly encouraging, for the most part. My wounding was primarily inflicted by unhealthy men, not women. However, I know that's not the case for everyone. I know many men who developed bisexual or homosexual arousal templates have been wounded just as deeply by females as males. That, I believe, only makes their emotional healing work more challenging.

A Further Biblical Perspective (Scott)

In the book of Genesis, it says simply, "So God created man in His own image; in the image of God He created him; male and female He created them" (Genesis 1:27).

Jesus quotes this passage in the New Testament in Matthew 19:4 and Mark 10:6. The idea that God made men and women different is found in both the New Testament and the Old Testament. Therefore, it is true that there are traits unique to masculinity as well as traits unique to femininity. Certainly, there is overlap between men and women (we are all human, and we share many common traits), but inherently there are differences, too. This book focuses on the traits that are specifically associated with men's need for masculinity, but I will also say that many of the traits that men ought to have can be seen in women in some form, too. It isn't that these traits are ONLY for men, but that masculine traits are NECESSARY for men.

What does biblical masculinity look like?

If we can identify masculine traits, we can begin to practice them ... and remember, practice is the goal, not perfection. Biblical masculinity is a journey for all men, an attempt to emulate that model of male behavior that God sets forth in His Word.

First and foremost, masculinity seeks to shape the world through work. The first task God gave to Adam was to "tend the garden and keep it" (Genesis 2:15). Biblical masculinity begins with finding worthwhile work that makes a mark on the world around us. When God made the Garden of Eden, it was already a perfect place, but God allowed, and even commanded, Adam to maintain and shape that garden after his own personality. The garden became Adam's area of dominion. It was his corner of the world to remake after his own image and to place his own particular fingerprint upon.

All men must seek a kingdom, an area of dominion that they can shape. Masculinity craves dominion. If it doesn't find a positive kingdom in which to rule as a servant-king, it is likely to show up in outbursts of tyranny instead. Every man must ask himself, "In what way am I improving the world and leaving my mark?" It may be in business, family, art, invention, charity, or a thousand other areas. From the plumber who finds satisfaction in saving someone's Thanksgiving by fixing an untimely clog to the small business owner who has created an operation that provides employment for a dozen people to the father who is raising the next generation to stand on a foundation he never had— these are all work and dominion behaviors that fulfill our desire for biblical masculinity.

Another common theme found in biblical representations of masculinity is "warrior" behaviors of sacrificial protection and service.

The need to guard and protect while also providing is essential to men. Warriors must have something to fight for. David conquered Goliath. Caleb and Joshua believed they could take the Promised Land. Samson repelled the Philistines and squelched the oppressors of Israel. Abraham saved his nephew, Lot, from a raiding army. Everywhere you look in the Bible you see men leading and willing to suffer for the lives of others. No man will truly be masculine until he has found some people to sacrifice for. It is the way of the warrior to put others before oneself, place oneself in harm's way, and stand against what is evil on behalf of those who are weaker.

Whether it be by serving with a charity, "caring for the widow and the fatherless in their distress" (James 1:27), or serving your spouse with sacrificial care, or taking on a cause of injustice in this world, men must find others to fight for. Men who have nothing to suffer for will find their masculinity suffering. All men need to practice warrior service. Guide, guard, and protect.

Another way in which masculinity is practiced is through craftsmanship. Proverbs 22:29 says, "Do you see a man skillful in his work? He will stand before kings; he will not stand before obscure men." The Bible is full of examples of men that made an impact because they were men of precision and craftsmanship. Bezalel and Oholiab were particularly skilled craftsmen that built the tabernacle with their abilities to work in wood, metal, and precious stones (see

Exodus 36:1). Solomon dedicated himself to wisdom, even to the point of becoming an expert in botany, horticulture, ornithology, and herpetology (see 1 Kings 4:33). Jesus was Himself a carpenter (see Mark 6:3).

Working with your hands and your mind to learn skills that others don't have is one way in which men exercise their masculinity. The curiosity to gain knowledge and become an expert in things is practicing biblical masculinity.

Far too many men fail to truly become masculine because they don't pursue excellence. The opposite of excellence is mediocrity—and it is truly hard to feel like a man when you feel mediocre. Those with same-sex attractions are often particularly vulnerable to the dangers of mediocrity. If a man experiences SSA, he often is already questioning his masculinity, and feelings of mediocrity or being "less than" swirl around him. One practice that can combat that is to find an area in which you can be a true craftsman. "Whatever your hand finds to do, do it with all your might" (Ecclesiastes 9:10).

And last, masculine men know how to feel deeply, enjoy life, and be creative. In today's culture, we are often taught that feelings are the antithesis of masculinity, but that is wildly incorrect. All men would do well to remember that the same David who was king and warrior was also "the sweet psalmist of Israel" (2 Samuel 23:1). David fought wars, commanded armies, ruled a flourishing kingdom, and wrote poetry. These things are not opposite; they are complementary.

Creativity and the ability to express emotion articulately are important aspects of manhood. Men must be able to love well. This is not just true romantically, but it is true in our relationships with our children, our parents, our friends, and even in our relationships with our enemies. The ability to express through speech, artwork, music, or writing are skills that may benefit any man. It will look different in each man, but things like writing in a journal, playing guitar, drawing, cooking, or even remodeling a home through DIY projects are all ways in which masculinity can be expressed through creativity.

Like all masculine traits, pursuing your passions can be taken to the extreme and to the unhealthy. However, when understood and practiced within the context of biblical ethics, emotional outlets and creative expression are clearly associated with the Creator's model of masculinity.

These four areas all provide a matrix for a biblical model of masculine practice:

1. *A king's dominion and pursuit of work*
2. *A warrior's sacrificial protection and service*
3. *A craftsman's pursuit of expertise and knowledge*
4. *An artist's pursuit of passion and emotional release*

CHAPTER 13: CONCLUSION & PLANS TO PROSPER

"For I Know the Plans I Have for You"

Jeremiah 29:11–14 tells us, "'*For I know the plans that I have for you,' declares the Lord, 'plans for welfare and not for calamity, to give you a future and a hope.* Then you will call upon Me and come and pray to Me, and I will listen to you. You will seek me and find Me when you search for me with all your heart. I will be found by you,' declares the Lord, 'and I will restore your fortunes and will gather you from all the nations and from all the places where I have driven you,' declares the Lord, 'and I will bring you back to the place from where I sent you into exile.'"

These verses were a message for the people of Israel who were in exile, foretelling of their future prosperity in seventy years' time. In the preceding verses, they were instructed to build a life for themselves even while they were in exile. How interesting, when I overlay that same concept onto my own journey, I have felt "in exile" throughout my lifetime, worried about people discovering the truth of my having a bisexual arousal template. As I sit here writing the conclusion of this book, I already feel that God's plan for me is being fulfilled with so much abundance. God does have a plan for me that is full of welfare and hope.

The title of this book references 2 Corinthians 5:7: "For we walk by faith; not by sight." I hope *Walk by Faith, Not by Sexuality* captures the idea that my faith in Christ has been my anchor all while wrestling and denying the undercurrent of the flesh. 2 Corinthians 5 focuses on the Temporal (or worldly) versus the Eternal. The words of the entire chapter, written by the apostle Paul and Timothy, speak directly to my soul, and are the exact closing message I'd like to share.

2 CORINTHIANS CHAPTER 5 (IN ITS ENTIRETY)

The Temporal and Eternal

¹ For we know that if our earthly tent which is our house is torn down, we have a building from God, a house not made by hands, eternal in the heavens. ² For indeed, in this *tent* we groan, longing to be clothed with our dwelling from heaven, ³ since in fact after putting it on, we will not be found naked. ⁴ For indeed, we who are in this tent groan, being burdened, because we do not want to be unclothed but to be clothed, so that what is mortal will be swallowed up by life. ⁵ Now He who prepared us for this very *purpose is* God, who gave us the Spirit as a pledge.

⁶ Therefore, being always of good courage, and knowing that while we are at home in the body we are absent from the Lord— ⁷ for we walk by faith, not by sight— ⁸ but we are of good courage and prefer rather to be absent from the body and to be at home with the Lord. ⁹ Therefore we

also have as our ambition, whether at home or absent, to be pleasing to Him. ¹⁰ For we must all appear before the judgment seat of Christ, so that each one may receive compensation for his deeds *done* through the body, in accordance with what he has done, whether good or bad.

¹¹ Therefore, knowing the fear of the Lord, we persuade people, but we are well-known to God; and I hope that we are also well-known in your consciences. ¹² We are not commending ourselves to you again, but *are* giving you an opportunity to be proud of us, so that you will have *an answer* for those who take pride in appearance and not in heart. ¹³ For if we have lost our minds, *it is* for God; if we are of sound mind, *it is* for you. ¹⁴ For the love of Christ controls us, having concluded this, that one died for all, therefore all died; ¹⁵ and He died for all, so that those who live would no longer live for themselves, but for Him who died and rose on their behalf.

¹⁶ Therefore from now on we recognize no one by the flesh; even though we have known Christ by the flesh, yet now we know *Him in this way* no longer. ¹⁷ Therefore if anyone is in Christ, *this person is* a new creation; the old things passed away; behold, new things have come. ¹⁸ Now all *these* things are from God, who reconciled us to Himself through Christ and gave us the ministry of reconciliation, ¹⁹ namely, that God was in Christ reconciling the world to Himself, not counting their wrongdoings against them, and He has committed to us the word of reconciliation.

[20] Therefore, we are ambassadors for Christ, as though God were making an appeal through us; we beg you on behalf of Christ, be reconciled to God. [21] He made Him who knew no sin *to be* sin in our behalf, so that we might become the righteousness of God in Him.

I am reconciled to God through Jesus, His Son, which has been so comforting to me. The goal of this journey, working with Scott, and developing the FB-AACP Therapy protocol, was to become reconciled with myself.

I love the photo of a man looking in the mirror and reflecting back is an image of himself as a child. My inner child has always been with me, fighting for his voice. I'd like to close by letting him step up to the podium.

Inner child, Terry:

"I want to thank you for giving me a voice, Terry. Throughout my life I've been so scared, but I'm not scared anymore. I release all the boys and all the men who intentionally or unintentionally hurt us. The friends who laughed at me in Larry's bedroom but had no idea how soul crushing that experience was for me due to my hidden attractions. Our father and brother were so angry. The captain who repeatedly berated us. I forgive them all just as Jesus, our savior, has forgiven us. I can also honestly say that I love them all, just as Jesus, our savior, loves us. The hardships did make us resilient.

"I'm no longer afraid of being called gay, or weak, or stupid. Because we're not. We are loved. We are loved by Jesus, Holly, the kids, our family, our friends, our tribe, and our church. I also know that Dad and Gary, who are no longer with us, loved us in their heart of hearts. I do look forward to the day that we will finally be able to go home to be with our Heavenly Father and to embrace Jesus who's been with us in our darkest moments. I am so glad that the suicide attempt was unsuccessful and that we had the opportunity to grow and heal. I no longer feel shame. We did the best we could. It's over and we are safe now. And we can now protect ourselves. God be the glory! We are at peace within. Now, can we go to McDonalds?"

Fully congruent adult/child, Terry

For those who took the time to read this book, thank you. I pray that God blesses you on your journey of congruency and inner peace.

Thank you to my brother Scott for his contributions to this book, his friendship and sound spiritual counsel for many years to come.

Thank you to my brother Rich for his friendship, writing the foreword and consulting on Brothers Road M.A.N.S. principles.

Thank you to all my brothers from Journey Into Manhood, Journey Continues, and Journey Beyond. The gift of being a witness to each other's work is forever in my heart.

I thank my mother for being there throughout my life with unconditional love.

I thank my wife, Holly, for being my rock, loving me, and giving us three beautiful children (Eliora, Izzy, and Joshua), who are all gifts from the one true God.

And foremost, I thank my Lord and Savior, Jesus. For hearing my prayer(s) as a child and never leaving my side throughout the years, even when in sin.

In the appendix you'll find a copy of the Advanced Informed Consent along with the worksheets I use when working with clients who want to incorporate the Faith-Based Acceptance, Abstinence, Congruency, and Practice Protocol into their counseling.

I want to thank Dr. Mark Yarhouse who so graciously allowed me to tailor the Advanced Informed Consent from his book titled Sexual Identity and Faith: Helping Client's Find Congruence.

APPENDIX A: ADVANCED INFORMED CONSENT

Faith-Based Acceptance, Abstinence, Congruency & Practice Therapy (for Pastoral and Christian Counselors' Consideration in practice)

(Adapted from the extended informed consent in Sexual Identity & Faith Helping Clients find Congruency by Dr. Mark Yarhouse)

THE CONTEXT OF THE FB-AACP THERAPY MODEL

THIS DOCUMENT SERVES AS A CONSENT FORM FOR INDIVIDUALS PARticipating in Faith-Based Acceptance, Abstinence, Congruency & Practice Therapy (FB-AACP Therapy). FB-AACP Therapy is an approach centered around biblical principles and identity exploration, with an emphasis on promoting healthy coping and social support. The goal of FB-AACP Therapy is to provide Christian men with a biblical framework for understanding their same-sex attractions, supporting their voluntary choice of abstinence from acting on these attractions, and simultaneously fostering increased self-acceptance and congruency.

It's important to note that FB-AACP Therapy does not aim to change sexual orientation itself or alter a person's sexual arousal template. Instead, the focus is on enhancing self-acceptance and congruency in a manner that aligns with the individual's circumstances and faith.

In the therapeutic process, informed consent is crucial, drawing from a consumer model of service delivery. This form provides background information as part of the informed consent process.

When discussing sexual identity, we refer to the labels that individuals use to perceive themselves and present to others. Sexual identity can be private (personal self-perception) or public (how one presents or is described by others). Common sexual identity labels include gay, straight, bi, bicurious, lesbian, same-sex attracted (SSA), questioning, and queer.

FB-AACP Therapy, in its current practice, emphasizes a biblical framework for Christians to navigate same-sex attractions in alignment with their religious beliefs, calling for abstinence from expressing these feelings in romantic or sexual relationships. Recognizing that people interpret their same-sex sexuality in various ways, FB-AACP Therapy aims to help individuals identify and reflect on the "stories" (meaning, personal narrative, framework) they tell themselves or hear from others in this context. These stories may influence expectations about the role of same-sex sexuality in one's life.

FB-AACP Therapy, being a Christian-based protocol, assists individuals in identifying and evaluating these "stories," seeking to create an accurate and meaningful narrative that aligns with their values and beliefs. Collaborating with a Pastoral or Christian counselor, individuals can develop a story, identity, or personal narrative supported by those who share similar beliefs, fostering social support in their journey of self-understanding. The ultimate goal is to help individuals identify and address concerns or conflicts they wish to explore in therapy.

This protocol is complementary to other therapeutic approaches across the mental health profession.

RECOMMENDED PROFESSIONAL APPROACHES

In 2009, an APA task force on appropriate therapeutic responses to sexual orientation acknowledged that some individuals may not be suitable candidates for gay affirmative therapy (GAT) as traditionally practiced. For instance, people may hold personal or religious beliefs that prevent them from engaging in GAT if the clinician already has a predetermined opinion on the best resolution for conflicts between faith and sexuality. In such instances, the APA recognizes that alternative therapeutic models that are client-centered and identity-focused, highlighting social support and healthy coping mechanisms while allowing exploration of conflicts between sexual and religious identities, may better serve the client.

To that end, Mark A. Yarhouse, Psy.D., author of *Sexual Identity & Faith: Helping Clients Find Congruence*, has developed a Sexual Identity Therapy (SIT) protocol that guides clients in exploring their sexual identity through various Christian perspectives, considered a recommended approach in the mental health community.

Before Sexual Identity Therapy, two contrasting approaches were prevalent: sexual orientation change efforts (SOCE) and gay affirmative therapy (GAT). Professional organizations have distanced themselves from, and criticized, SOCE and its aim of helping clients shift toward a heterosexual orientation—a goal widely discouraged due to doubts about its effectiveness and the understanding that homosexuality is not a mental illness (as recognized by major mental health organizations like the American Psychological Association [APA] and the American Psychiatric Association).

In contrast, GAT focuses on integrating same-sex sexuality into both private and public identity, along with corresponding intimate relationships. While not a specific therapy protocol, GAT serves as a lens for individuals to navigate being gay, often leading to tensions with traditional religious beliefs. Recognizing the value of providing a safe environment to explore such tensions, Dr. Yarhouse developed Sexual Identity Therapy, which is client-centered and identity-focused, emphasizing healthy coping and social support. Importantly, SIT does not prescribe a predetermined outcome for the client's sexual identity or define what achieving congruence means in the context of the client's beliefs and values.

FB-AACP Therapy, a subset of Christian viewpoints within Sexual Identity Therapy, aligns with the belief that orientation change may not (and need not) be expected, yet individuals may still have moral concerns about same-gender attractions and practices. Those following FB-AACP Therapy typically refrain from using identity labels like "gay" or "queer" and may disidentify with aspects of the mainstream LGBTQ+ community. In my reading, this perspective also aligns with the Christian thought found in the book *Holy Sexuality and the Gospel* by Christopher Yuan, DMin.

FB-AACP Therapy caters to Christians who enter therapy with the goal of abstaining from acting on expressions of same-sex attraction while aiming to enhance personal acceptance and congruency with their values and beliefs. Emphasizing freedom of choice (free will), FB-AACP Therapy provides a biblical lens to view same-sex attraction and a protocol to support and build a client's narrative based on their Christian values and lived experience.

As mental health care models increasingly shift toward evidence-based practices, it is crucial to note that there is a lack of well-designed outcome studies addressing conflicts or concerns related to sexual and religious identity. This means that, ideally, therapeutic approaches should be based on empirical research demonstrating the likely results of the chosen approach. However, none of the existing approaches in this realm—whether SOCE, GAT, or client-affirmative/sexual identity approaches like SIT or FB-AACP Therapy—have been extensively researched in terms of outcomes.

A COLLABORATIVE APPROACH TO FB-AACP THERAPY

The overarching aim of FB-AACP Therapy is to support you in achieving greater acceptance, endorsing your decision for abstinence from engaging in same-sex behaviors, providing a biblical perspective to your lived experience, enhancing social support and congruence, all while accommodating your faith practice. Specific goals within this approach can vary among individuals, but commonly include:

- Identifying and addressing co-occurring concerns, such as depression or anxiety

- Constructing a personal and biblical narrative that reflects congruence

- Recognizing and engaging in healthy coping activities

- Expanding social support in alignment with your vision of congruence

- Disclosing same-sex sexuality to family and others

- Improving strained family and other relationships that may have resulted from the disclosure of same-sex sexuality

The existence of informed consent is crucial to ensure that you can make well-informed decisions regarding your treatment goals and the available services. If you discover that you are not making significant progress within this approach, it is important, as with any other therapeutic method, to revisit your goals and reassess whether the program itself aligns with your specific needs.

POTENTIAL BENEFITS/ RISKS/OUTCOMES WITH OR WITHOUT THERAPY

Beyond concerns related to sexual identity, individuals I work with often bring up various co-occurring issues. These issues can be diverse, encompassing depressed mood, anxiety, and conflicts within families. I make a concerted effort to identify and address these concerns early in our discussions. I find that addressing these issues early on is beneficial because it allows clients to make decisions about their sexual identity from a more stable and normal mood state, as opposed to making decisions in a state of depression, for example. This underscores one potential advantage of therapy. Even if you ultimately determine that FB-AACP Therapy is not the right fit for you, I may recommend pursuing therapy with another professional to address any co-occurring issues.

Another potential positive outcome of therapy is the resolution of sexual identity conflicts, often referred to as achieving congruence. Congruence, in this context, involves living and shaping an identity that aligns with your beliefs and values. While I am not aware of any specific risks associated with pursuing therapy to address these concerns, it's important to acknowledge that any therapy involves both an emotional and financial commitment.

CONSENT TO FAITH-BASED ACCEPTANCE, ABSTINENCE, CONGRUENCY & PRACTICE THERAPY

I have thoroughly reviewed this document, discussed its contents with my therapist or pastoral couselor, and hereby agree to the terms outlined. By providing this authorization, I acknowledge my informed consent for participation in Faith-Based Acceptance, Abstinence, Congruency, and Practice Therapy. A photocopy or facsimile of this form, including my signature, will be regarded as a valid representation of my consent.

Patient Signature:

____Date:____________

Therapist/Pastoral Counselor Signature:

____Date:____________

Faith-Based Acceptance, Abstinence, Congruency & Practice Therapy Worksheets for Christian & Pastoral Counselors

(ROADMAP)

Biblical Masculinity vs.
Tyrannical Masculinity

1 COR 16:13–14

*"Be on the alert, stand firm in the faith, act like men, be
strong. Let all that you do be done in love."*

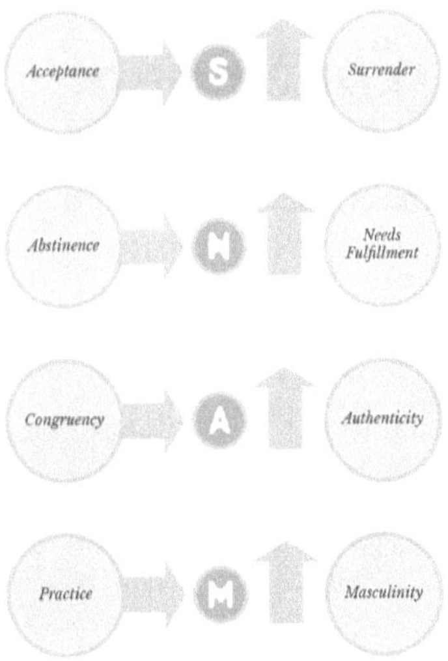

The FB-AACP® pillars and the M.A.N.S.® principles are, in many respects, complementary areas of focus, with the FB-AACP framework focused more on biblical concepts and terminology and the M.A.N.S. principles focused more on underlying emotional work.

Together, they can lead men to live more authentically and congruently with their faith, values, beliefs, and life goals.

ACCEPTANCE

God loves and **accepts** us just as we are!
(Romans 15:7; 1 Timothy 1:15)

ABSTINENCE

God calls us to **abstain** from fleshly lusts
which wage war against the soul.
(1 Peter 2:11; 1 Thessalonians 4:3)

CONGRUENCY

God calls us to live in **congruency** by confessing
our struggles and sharing our burdens.
(Acts 19:18; 2 Corinthians 12:9–10)

PRACTICE

God calls us to **practice** (not to perfect)
truth, light, and righteousness.
(John 3:21; 1 John 3:7)

WORKSHEETS ON ACCEPTANCE

God loves and **accepts** us just as we are!
(Romans 15:7; 1 Timothy 1:15)

Romans 15:7 says: "Therefore, accept one another, just as Christ also accepted us to the glory of God."

1 Timothy 1:15 adds, "It is a trustworthy statement, deserving full acceptance, that Christ Jesus came into the world to save sinners, among whom I am foremost of all."

There is little doubt from the message of scripture that we are called and accepted into the Kingdom of God in spite of our imperfections. Identify your barriers to acceptance below.

Q: How much do you feel accepted by God? 0–100% ________

Describe a time you felt accepted by God.

Describe a time you felt rejected by God.

Q: How much do you feel accepted by yourself (self-acceptance)?
0–100% ________

Describe a time you felt accepted by yourself.

Describe a time you felt rejected by yourself.

Q: How much do you feel you would be accepted by your church if they knew   your struggles? 0–100% __________

Describe a time you felt accepted by your church.

Describe a time you felt rejected by your church.

Q: If you belonged to a church who knew your struggles with same-sex attractions and felt accepted 100%, with hearts of bearing one another's burdens, how would that impact your sense of self-acceptance and feelings of being accepted by God?

Acceptance by Church: 100%

The impact it would have with feelings of acceptance by God? 0–100% __________

The impact it would have with feelings of self-acceptance? 0–100% __________

What might you need to change within yourself in order to feel more accepted by your church community?

Are there ways you could help your church community to become more accepting and supportive of those who struggle with same-sex attractions and who seek to abstain from acting on those attractions in order to be in alignment with biblical teachings?

____

____

____

____

____

____

____

____

Now let's examine your beliefs to explain, through a biblical lens, why you might have same-sex attractions?

- Do you believe that your SSA may have come about largely because God allowed the natural consequences of forbidden sexual thoughts and behaviors to lead you to greater levels of homoeroticism? (See chapter 7, page 49.)

Romans 1: 24–27 says,

²⁴ Therefore God gave them over in the lusts of their hearts to impurity, so that their bodies would be dishonored among them. ²⁵ For they exchanged the truth of God for a lie, and worshiped and served the creature rather than the Creator, who is blessed forever. Amen.

²⁶ For this reason God gave them over to degrading passions; for their women exchanged the natural function for that which is unnatural, ²⁷ and in the same way also the men abandoned the natural function of the woman and burned in their desire toward one another, men with men committing indecent acts and receiving in their own persons the due penalty of their error.

If so, what milestone experiences or behaviors have led you to the belief that your SSA came about because God allowed you to turn your mind over to lust?

____

____

____

Ecclesiastes 9:11 says,

¹¹ I again saw under the sun that the race is not to the swift and the battle is not to the warriors, and neither is bread to the wise nor wealth to the discerning nor favor to men of ability; for time and chance overtake them all.

- Do you believe your SSA came about randomly, by happenstance? (See chapter 7, page 49.)

____

____

____

Matthew 5: 43–44 says,

43 "You have heard that it was said, 'YOU SHALL LOVE YOUR NEIGHBOR and hate your enemy.' 44 But I say to you, love your enemies and pray for those who persecute you, 45 so that you may [ap]be sons of your Father who is in heaven; for He causes His sun to rise on *the* evil and *the* good, and sends rain on *the* righteous and *the* unrighteous.

If so, what milestone experiences or behaviors have led you to the belief that your SSA came about by happenstance?

____

____

____

- Do you believe you were chosen by God to experience SSA as part of your mortal challenges?

____

____

____

Psalms 139:13–16 says,

> For You formed my inward parts; You wove me in my
> mother's womb. [14] I will give thanks to You, for I am fear-
> fully and wonderfully made; Wonderful are Your works,
> And my soul knows it very well.

If so, what milestone experiences have led you to the belief that
you were chosen to experience SSA?

____

____

____

Note: It is not uncommon for Christians to believe they fall into
the category of God turning their minds over to lust if they have
a history of pornography exploration that may have led to an addiction. If a pornography addiction is present, it may require a
treatment protocol focused on regaining self-control. A treatment
protocol for compulsive sex addiction can run concurrent with the
FB-AACP Therapy protocol.

See Appendix D where I share treatment options that I present to clients to treat a sex addiction.

WORKSHEETS ON SURRENDER

The concept of surrendering to God's will is interwoven with the principle of acceptance of self and acceptance of God's sovereignty in our lives.

The following questions are designed to encourage deeper reflection on the themes of surrender presented in FB-AACP Therapy and may provide a starting point for meaningful therapeutic exploration.

- **Awareness and Exploration:**

  - Can you identify any areas in your life where you feel resistant to change, especially in terms of aligning your natural desires with spiritual principles?

  ____

  ____

  ____

  - What are the internal resistances or blocks that you recognize in yourself? How do this manifest in your thoughts and behaviors?

  ____

  ____

  ____

- **Facing Challenges:**

  - Can you recall specific instances where you faced challenges in surrendering to the path of healing and growth?

  ____

  ____

  ____

  - How do you deal with the tension between desiring positive change and resisting the hard work it entails?

  ____

  ____

  ____

- **Rejecting "Shoulds" and Accepting Reality:**

  - In what ways have you struggled with the concept of accepting reality as it is rather than how you think it should be?

  ____

  ____

  ____

- How does the idea of letting go of the "shoulds" and accepting the world as it is resonated with you?

____

____

____

- Renewal and Inner Conflict:

- How do you approach the process of daily renewal in your life? What practices or rituals help you become willing to let God change you from within?

____

____

____

Romans 8: 26–27 says,

In the same way the Spirit also helps our weakness; for we do to know how to pray as we should, but the Spirit Himself intercedes for us with groanings too deep words; and He who searches the hearts knows what the mind of the Spirit is, because He intercedes for the saints according to the will of God.

- Can you share an experience when God's spirit searched the groaning of your soul during prayer?

- **Redirecting Self-Will:**

  - How do you notice the impact of self-will on your overall contentment and alignment with God's will?

  - What does it mean for you to redirect your thinking, fears, resentments, and desires toward alignment with God?

- **Authentic Submission:**

  - How do you authentically submit your desires to God's will, especially in areas where you find it challenging?

  ____

  ____

  ____

  - Can you recall a specific moment when asking God to change your rebellious heart had a noticeable impact on your life?

  ____

  ____

  ____

- **Acknowledging Desires:**

  - How do you balance acknowledging your desires, including sinful ones, while surrendering them over to God?

  ____

  ____

  ____

- What role does authenticity play in this process of acknowledging desires and seeking alignment with God?

____

____

____

- **Letting Go of Harmful Attachments:**

  - Which harmful thoughts, behaviors, or relationships do you find most challenging to release your attachments to?

  ____

  ____

  ____

  - How has releasing these attachments contributed to a more peaceful and less conflicted life for you?

  ____

  ____

  ____

2 Corinthians 10:5 says

⁵ We are destroying speculations, and every lofty thing raised up against the knowledge of God, and we are taking every through captive to the obedience of Christ.

- How would releasing your attachments to harmful thoughts affect your desire and ability to "take captive every thought to make it obedient to Christ" ?

____

____

____

- **Spiritual Work and Surrendering to God:**

  - Reflecting on your journey, how have you approached the difficult spiritual work of accepting and forgiving, especially regarding incongruent same-sex attractions?

____

____

____

  - Can you share a specific experience of releasing dependence on lust as a coping mechanism through surrender to God?

____

____

____

- **Sexual Identity and Arousal Template:**

  - How has your understanding of sexual identity, sexual expression, and arousal templates evolved over time?

  ____

  ____

  ____

  - In what ways do you integrate your outward Christian heterosexual identity with the internal incongruence of same-sex attractions?

  ____

  ____

  ____

WORKSHEETS ON ABSTINENCE

God calls us to **abstain** from fleshly lusts which wage war against the soul.

- **Personal Meaning of Abstinence:**

1 Peter 2:11 says,.

"Beloved, I urge you as aliens and strangers to abstain from fleshly lusts which wage war against the soul."

- How do you personally define abstinence for yourself, especially in the context of 1 Peter 2:11?

____

____

____

- In what ways has the concept of abstaining from fleshly lusts impacted your journey with Christ?

____

____

____

- **Chosen by Christ**

1 Peter 2:9-10 says,

But you are a CHOSE RACE, a ROYAL PRIEST-HOOD, a HOLY NATION, A PEOPLE FOR GOD'S OWN POSSESSION, so that you may proclaim the excellencies of Him who has called you out of darkness into His marvelous light; for you once were NOT A PEOPLE, but now you are THE PEOPLE OF GOD; you had NOT RECEIVED MERCY, but now you have RECEIVED MERCY.

- Reflecting on 1 Peter 2:9–10, how has your understanding of being chosen, desired, affirmed, wanted, and accepted by Christ influenced your healing process?

____

____

____

- Can you identify specific moments where you felt the healing power of these affirmations in your life?

____

____

____

- **Past Experiences and Abstinence:**

  - Consider your experiences in engaging in sexual experiences outside of your values and beliefs. How did or how have those experiences impacted you emotionally and spiritually?

  ____

  ____

  ____

  - In what ways has abstinence from such experiences contributed to your sense of sanctification and spiritual well-being?

  ____

  ____

  ____

- **God's Will for Sanctification:**

1 Thessalonians 4:3-7 notes:

For this is the will of God, your sanctification; that is, that you abstain from sexual immorality; that each of you know how to possess his own vessel in sanctification and honor, not in lustful passion, like the Gentiles who do not know God; and that no man transgress and defraud his brother in the matter because the Lord is the avenger in all these things, just as we also told you before and solemnly warned you. For God has not called us for the purpose of impurity, but in sanctification.

- How do you interpret and personally connect with 1 Thessalonians 4:3–7 and its emphasis on God's will for sanctification through abstaining from sexual immorality?

____

____

____

- Can you share instances where abstinence has played a role in your ongoing process of sanctification?

____

____

____

- **Abstaining from Lustful Passion:**

  - How do you navigate the challenges of abstaining from lustful passion, especially in contrast to the behaviors of those who do not know God?

____

____

____

- In what ways has this principle influenced your understanding of honor and sanctification?

WORKSHEETS ON NEEDS FULFILLMENT

One of the most powerful ways to increase our ability and desire to abstain from unrighteous thoughts and behaviors is to explore and discover our underlying, authentic needs that those sinful behaviors may be covering up.

I find that the Brothers Road organization's emphasis on meeting core needs can make us healthier, more fulfilled men who are much less inclined to turn to unhealthy distractions.

Please rate 1–5, with 1 being the lowest and 5 the highest, how satisfied you are that you are sufficiently meeting these needs in your current life. Then circle the top three needs that are most important to you.

1. I like, accept, and respect myself. _______

2. I have meaningful, supportive friendships with men who are like **brothers** to me. ______

3. I belong to at least one **"tribe"** of family, friends, and communities who work together toward common goals and who support each other in becoming better people. ______

4. I have people in my life who **I love** deeply, and I know **I am loved** likewise loved by others. ______

5. I hold beliefs and values that **anchor** me to truth and purpose. ______

6. I engage my body in positive **physical work and activities** that energize and uplift me. ______

7. I structure my life so that I am continually **challenged** and always learning, growing, and stretching my limits. ______

8. My life has a **mission** or purpose. ______

Self-Love and Self-Perception:

Romans7:24–25 says,

> Wretched man that I am! Who will set me free from the body of this death? Thanks be to God through Jesus Christ our Lord! So then, on the one hand I myself with my mind am serving the law of God, but on the other, with my flesh the law of sin"

- Reflecting on Paul's struggle in Romans 7, how do you perceive yourself when you contemplate your past mistakes or shortcomings?

____

____

____

- In what ways does the knowledge of Jesus' sacrifice help you in developing self-respect and self-acceptance?

____

____

____

- **Balancing Knowledge and Emotion:**

    - How do you balance the intellectual knowledge that God loves you with the emotional aspects of liking, accepting, and respecting yourself?

    ____

    ____

    ____

    - Are there specific practices or perspectives that help bridge the gap between knowing God's love and feeling a sense of self-worth?

    ____

    ____

    ____

- **Brotherhood and Authentic Bonds:**

    1 Samuel 18:1 says,

    Not it came about when he had finished speaking to Saul, that the soul of Jonathan was knit to the soul of David, and Jonathan loved him as himself.

- In the context of David and Jonathan's friendship, what qualities do you believe are essential for authentic brotherhood or friendships?

____

____

____

- How can you ensure that your relationships align with spiritual values and contribute positively to your life?

____

____

____

- **Quality over Quantity:**

Proverbs 18:24 says,

A man of too many friends comes to ruin, but there is a friend who sticks closer than a brother.

- How do you interpret this scripture in terms of your need for brotherhood?

____

____

____

- Are there instances where you've experienced the importance of quality bonds over a larger circle of acquaintances?

____

____

____

- On the other hand, have you found if you put too much emphasis on a particular individual friendship that you could be at risk of becoming obsessed or even falling in love?

____

____

____

- How can you navigate these potential extremes in building godly friendships?

____

____

____

- **Church and Tribe:**

Hebrews 10:24-25 says,

And let us consider how to stimulate one another to love and good deeds, not forsaking our own assembling together, as is the habit of some, but encouraging one another; and all the more, as you see the day drawing near.

1 Corinthians 12:12 says,

For even as the body is one and yet has many members, and all the members of the body, though they are many, are one body, so also is Christ.

- How do you view your church community in terms of being a family and a tribe, as described in Hebrews and Corinthians?

____

____

____

- In what ways has your involvement in the church positively impacted your sense of belonging and strength?

____

____

____

- **Diversity in the Church:**

  - Reflect on the idea that the church is designed by God to include people from different backgrounds (for instance, in Paul's "body of Christ" metaphor in 1 Corinthians 12.) How has diversity enriched your experience within the church?

    ____

    ____

    ____

  - Are there specific instances where the diversity within your church community has been a source of strength and support? Do you know any other Christians who experience same-sex attraction in the church, and who are open about their choice of abstinence?

    ____

    ____

    ____

- **Infatuation or Love:**

  - Drawing parallels with Samson's seeking of love with harlots, how have you pursued love in your life? (See Judges 16.)

    ____

    ____

    ____

- In what ways can the need for love sometimes lead individuals toward unhealthy relationships, and how can this be navigated?

____

____

____

- **Importance of Hope:**

Romans 8:24-25 says,

For in hope, we have been saved, but hope that is seen is not hope; for why does one also hope for what he sees? But if we hope for what we do not see, with perseverance we wait eagerly for it.

- How do you personally connect hope with salvation and anchoring the soul?

____

____

____

- Can you share instances where maintaining hope has been crucial in staving off discouragement and persevering through challenges?

____

____

____

- **Physical Activity and Challenge:**

Genesis 2:15 says,

> The LORD God took the man and put him in the Garden of Eden to work it and take care of it.

- Reflect on the idea that humans find purpose in physical labor. How does your work or engagement in physical activities contribute to your sense of purpose?

____

____

____

- Are there ways you can incorporate more physical activity into your life to address modern challenges like sleep disorders, depression, and anxiety?

____

____

____

- **Embracing Challenges:**

  - How comfortable are you with being challenged physically and spiritually?

  ____

  ____

  ____

  - Can you recall instances where overcoming challenges has positively impacted your sense of accomplishment and self-worth?

  ____

  ____

  ____

- **Mission and Purpose:**

John 12:27 says,

> Now My soul has become troubled; and what shall I say, 'Father, save Me from this hour'? But for this purpose, I came to this hour.

- Reflecting on Jesus' sense of purpose, how do you identify your mission or purpose in life?

____

____

____

- Are there specific goals or aspirations that drive you and provide a sense of why you endure challenges?

____

____

____

- **Dealing with Deceptions:**

  - In a culture that often ties sexual desires to one's purpose, how do you look toward a higher calling?

____

____

____

- Can you articulate your understanding of the mission described in the Scriptures and how it differs from the cultural narrative?

____

____

____

WORKSHEETS ON CONGRUENCY

Acts 19:18 says,

Many also of those who had believed kept coming, confessing and disclosing their practices.

- **Congruency and Vulnerability:**

  - Reflecting on Acts 19:18, how does the idea of confessing and disclosing practices resonate with you in your journey toward healing and authenticity?

---

2 Corinthians 12:9-10 says,

And he said to me, "My grace is sufficient for you, for power is perfected in weakness" Most gladly, therefore, I will rather boast about my weaknesses, so that the power of Christ may dwell in me. Therefore, I am well content with weaknesses, with insults, with distresses, with persecutions, for Christ's sake: for when I am weak, then I am strong.

- In 2 Corinthians12:9-10, Paul talks about boasting in weaknesses to let the power of Christ dwell. How comfortable are you in being open about your vulnerabilities and weaknesses in your faith community?

  ____

  ____

  ____

- **Intersection of Faith and Personal Journey:**

  - Share your experience (if any) disclosing your same-sex attractions with your spouse or partner. What would it be like to be fully known in a relationship while being faithful to your vows and remaining totally committed to one another.

  ____

  ____

  ____

  - Reflect on the love you have received and given to your spouse or partner. In what ways does this align with biblical teachings on love and acceptance, and how does it contribute to your ongoing journey of alignment with family?

  ____

  ____

  ____

- **The Power of Openness:**

  - How does the concept of "getting real to heal" impact your understanding of being consistent, both in your personal life and in your faith journey?

  ____

  ____

  ____

  - Share your thoughts on the idea that what might seem "vulnerable" could be viewed as an expression of love, truth, and encouragement to others.

  ____

  ____

  ____

  - How would the freedom of being congruent in your faith community impact your ability to be live congruently in other areas of life?

  ____

  ____

  ____

- **Seeking Support and Building Community:**

  - Describe your experience reaching out to your church leadership to share your journey, especially regarding same-sex attraction.

  ____

  ____

  ____

  - How did (or would) their response influence your sense of acceptance and belonging?

  ____

  ____

  ____

- **Alignment with Spiritual Authority:**

  - How does church leadership influence your spiritual and emotional wellness?

  ____

  ____

  ____

1 Timothy 5: 17 says,

The elders who rule well are to be considered worthy of double honor, especially those who work hard at preaching and teaching.

- How does (or how would) church leaderships acceptance and encouragement align with your understanding of spiritual leadership?

WORKSHEETS ON AUTHENTICITY

- **Acknowledging and Owning Personal Struggles:**

Romans 3:23 says,

> For all have sinned and fall short of the glory of God.

- Reflect on the idea that individuals with same-sex attractions may have grown up wearing a mask to hide their true selves. Based on Romans 3:23, would it be a safe assumption that all people wear a mask to some extent?

____

____

____

- **Exploring Coping Mechanisms:**

Psalm 34:18 says,

> The Lord is near to the brokenhearted and saves the crushed in spirit.

- Consider the coping mechanisms mentioned, such as escaping into fantasy. Have you ever used similar strategies to cope with difficult emotions or feelings of unworthiness?

____

____

____

- **Embracing Rigorous Authenticity:**

Ephesians 4:25 says,

> Therefore, having put away falsehood, let each one of you speak the truth with his neighbor, for we are members of one another.

- In what ways do you resonate with the concept of "getting real to heal"? How does rigorous authenticity align with the biblical principles of transparency and honesty?

____

____

____

- **Overcoming Shame through Transparency:**

Proverbs 28:13 says,

> Whoever conceals his transgressions will not prosper, but he who confesses and forsakes them will obtain mercy.

- Reflect on the role of shame and its impact on authentic living. How might transparency with trusted others help in overcoming shame?

____

____

____

- **Facing and Feeling Core Emotions:**

Psalm 51:10 says,

Create in me a clean heart, O God, and renew a right spirit within me.

- Discuss the importance of feeling authentic core emotions, like fear, anger, sadness, and love. How does this align with the biblical understanding of facing and processing emotions?

____

____

____

- **Healing Old Wounds and Pursuing Growth:**

Psalm 34:19 says,

Many are the afflictions of the righteous, but the Lord delivers him out of them all.

- Share your thoughts on pursuing personal growth and inner healing. How does this align with your understanding of the struggles in life, and your spiritual and emotional journey?

____

____

____

- **Living a Life of Service and Purpose:**

Matthew 20:28 says,

> Even as the Son of Man came not to be served but to serve, and to give His life as a ransom for many.

- Reflect on the impact of a life of service and purpose. How does this resonate with the idea that our wounds can become a source of our greatest gifts to the world?

- **Avoiding Hypocrisy and Living Authentically:**

Matthew 23:27 says,

> Woe to you, scribes and Pharisees, hypocrites! For you are like whitewashed tombs, which outwardly appear beautiful, but within are full of dead people's bones and all uncleanness.

- Explore the concept of hypocrisy and inauthentic living discussed in Matthew 23. How does living authentically align with the teachings of Jesus, who condemned hypocrisy?

- **Encouraging Others through Authenticity:**

2 Corinthians 1:3-4 says,

> Blessed be the God and Father of our Lord Jesus Christ, the Father of mercies and God of all comfort, who comforts us in all our affliction, so that we may be able to comfort those who are in any affliction, with the comfort with which we ourselves are comforted by God.

- Consider the impact on others of sharing their struggles openly. How can your authenticity serve as an encouragement to those who may be facing similar challenges?

____

____

____

WORKSHEETS ON PRACTICE

- **Acknowledging the Practice of Righteousness:**

Philippians 3:21 says,

> Not that I have already obtained this or am already perfect, but I press on to make it my own because Christ Jesus has made me His own.

- Reflect on the distinctions between practicing righteousness and being perfect in righteousness. How does understanding the concept of practice provide room for growth and improvement in one's journey of faith?

____

____

____

- **Understanding the Importance of Practice:**

Hebrews 5:14 says,

> But solid food is for the mature, for those who have their powers of discernment trained by constant practice to distinguish good from evil.

- Explore the significance of practicing righteousness in the context of personal growth. How does the idea of regularly exercising righteousness contribute to spiritual development?

____

____

____

- **Balancing Struggle and Righteous Living:**

James 1: 2-4 says,

> Consider it all joy, my brethren, when you encounter various trials, for you know that the testing of your faith produces steadfastness. And let steadfastness have its full effect, that you may be perfect and complete, lacking nothing.

- Acknowledge that struggling doesn't mean failure in the pursuit of righteousness. How can the understanding of ongoing struggles coexisting with righteous practices foster resilience in the journey of faith?

____

____

____

- **The Lifelong Journey of Emotional Healing:**

Psalm 147:3 says,

> He heals the brokenhearted and binds up their wounds.

- Consider the idea that emotional healing is a lifelong process. How does practicing righteousness contribute to the emotional work needed for healing from past wounds?

____

____

____

- **Community Support and Shared Struggles:**

Ecclesiastes 4: 9-10 says,

> Two are better than one because they have a good reward for their toil. For if they fall, one will lift up his fellow. But woe to him who is alone when he falls and has not another to lift him up!

- Explore the role of community in the journey of practicing righteousness. How does sharing struggles with others enhance the collective pursuit of sexual integrity?

____

____

____

- **Guarding against Spiritual Adversaries:**

Ephesians 6:11 says,

> Put on the whole armor of God, that you may be able to stand against the schemes of the devil.

- Explore the idea that practicing righteousness involves spiritual vigilance. How can individuals remain sober-spirited and on alert against the adversary while actively practicing right living?

WORKSHEETS ON MASCULINITY

- **Connecting to Our Own Masculinity:**

- **Biblical Masculinity:**

1Corinthians 16:13-14 says,

> Be on the alert, stand firm in the faith, act like men, be strong. Let all that you do be done in love.

- Discuss the concept of biblical masculinity presented in 1 Corinthians 16:13–14. How does the biblical definition of masculinity differ from with worlds view of masculinity?

____

____

____

Genesis 1:27 says,

> God created man in His own image, in the image of God He created him: male and female He created them.

- *Reflection on Genesis 1:27:* How does understanding that we are created in the image of God influence your perception of your own masculinity? How can acknowledging this contribute to a healthier self-view?

____

____

____

- *Work and Dominion:* In what ways are you currently engaging in worthwhile work, whether professionally or through volunteer service, that allow you to shape your world? How can you further seek a kingdom, an area of dominion, that might better align with your skills and passions?

____

____

____

- *Warrior Behavior:* Reflect on the concept of godly warriors having something to fight for. What or who are you currently fighting for in your life? How does having a purpose to protect and provide contribute to your sense of masculinity?

____

____

____

Proverbs 22:29 says,

Do you see a man skilled in his work? He will stand before kings; He will not stand before obscure men.

- *Craftsmanship:* Consider the idea of being skillful in your work. How are you actively pursuing excellence and expertise in your field or areas of interest? How does craftsmanship contribute to a sense of biblical masculinity?

____

____

____

- *Emotional Release and Creativity:* In what ways are you expressing your emotions and creativity? How can you further explore avenues such as writing, music, art, or DIY projects to enhance your emotional well-being and creative expression?

____

____

____

- **Bonding as Brothers with Other Men (Feeling Like "One of the Guys"):**

  - *Risk and Inclusion:* How open are you to including yourself in the world of men in new ways? What internal barriers or past experiences might be influencing your ability to connect with other men?

  ____

  ____

  ____

  - *Same-Sex Emotional Wounds:* Reflect on any emotional wounds related to same-sex interactions. How can you address and heal from these wounds to develop trust and connection with other men?

  ____

  ____

  ____

  - *Building Male Communities:* How can you actively contribute to or build meaningful male communities in your life? What shared goals or activities could help you establish a sense of belonging with other men?

  ____

  ____

  ____

- *Developing Platonic Friendships:* Evaluate your current relationships with male peers. Are there opportunities to develop multiple, meaningful, platonic friendships with other men? How can you broaden your circle of close male peers?

____

____

____

- *Mentoring Relationships:* Consider the qualities you admire in other men. How can you initiate mentoring relationships with men who can guide and support your growth? In what areas of your life would mentorship be particularly beneficial?

____

____

____

- **Developing Healthier Relationships with Women:**

Genesis 2:15 says,

Then the Lord God took the man and put him into the garden of Edenn to cultivate it and keep it.

- *Reflection on Genesis 2:15:* How does understanding the complementary nature of male and female roles, as seen in God's command to Adam, influence your approach to relationships with women?

\
\
\

- *Inner-Healing Work:* Reflect on any opposite-sex wounds you may carry. How can you engage in inner-healing work to address and overcome any unhealthy patterns or beliefs related to women?

\
\
\

- *Respecting Differences:* How can you cultivate a mindset that respects women as different but equal, recognizing their strengths, weaknesses, pain, and gifts? In what ways can you contribute to healthier dynamics in your relationships with women?

\
\
\

- *Grounded Masculine Energy:* Explore ways to remain grounded in your masculine energy in interactions with women. How can you maintain a healthy balance between your masculine qualities and the ability to relate to women with respect and understanding?

____

____

____

- *Romancing and Marriage:* If married, how can you actively engage in romancing your spouse? If single, how can you shift your focus from societal expectations to accepting yourself as a whole and complete man, regardless of marital status?

____

____

____

- **Celebrating Masculinity through Righteousness:**

1 Corinthians 16:14 says,

Let all that you do be done in Love.

- What are your goals for letting all you do being done in Love?

Terry's experience at Brother's Road's Journey into Manhood (JiM) Weekend

THE FOLLOWING IS A DESCRIPTION OF THE JiM WEEKEND FROM Brothers Road's website:

Journey into Manhood is a 48-hour immersion in intensive **self-discovery and personal-growth work.** The program is built around issues that are most common among men who experience distress or internal conflict over their same-sex attractions. Like not feeling "man enough." Or not "one of the guys." Or an unmet yearning for male attention, acceptance, and affirmation. Confusion over what it even means to be a man in today's world. Confusion and distress in relationships with women.

We create a highly supportive yet challenging environment for men to address these and related issues. **Men who do NOT experience sexual or romantic same-sex attractions also attend** Journey into Manhood and experience many of these same benefits working through these issues.

Journey into Manhood is an experiential weekend. You won't just sit and listen. You'll actively participate, connect, and explore. We create opportunities for you to experience healing, growth, and brotherhood, not just talk about them. More information concerning the weekend can be found at the following link: https://brothersroad.org/jim-about/.

I have heard it said within the mental health profession that an intensive weekend can be equivalent to 6 months to 1 year in therapy. I have no data to back that up, but for me this was exactly right. The best way I can explain the JiM weekend (from my experience) is that it was a healthy "rite of passage" into manhood, which felt so absent from my childhood. The weekend was hosted on a Christian campsite in a beautiful setting surrounded by nature.

I watched all the available videos on the Brothers Road website prior to registering to attend. I noted the benefits described from one former participant in a *20/20 News* segment on the Brothers Road website, which detailed one participant's experience, and one complaint from one former participant toward the end of that segment. The link to the video can be found here: https://brothersroad.org/videos/.

On the JiM weekend, we were broken up into smaller tribes of five or six men to complete deeper intensive work. This intensive work involved reenacting a self-selected childhood trauma in a process of psychodrama. For me, this was incredibly powerful as I selected to reenact the childhood trauma of what occurred at my friend's house when I was 13 prior to attempting suicide. One brother took on the role of God, standing on a chair, while repeating reassuring phrases which I chose during the reenactment, "I love and accept you," "Everything is going to be OK," and "I have a plan for you." I addressed my worst fears of being labeled "gay" during the psychodrama with an empowering ending, which in many respects overwrote the childhood event with a new memory. The facilitator's decision to have one of the tribe members roleplay God standing on a chair during the reenactment (for me) was brilliant as it served as a reminder that God was with me during my darkest hour. Looking back at how my life has unfolded leaves me no doubt of that now. Psychodrama can be quite intense, but it was more effective with addressing my childhood trauma than anything I'd experienced in the past.

Later that evening, back in the large group, I participated in another experiential exercise called the Golden Father Embrace. Participants were invited to select a staff member or another participant to hold them while an affirming song played in the background. Staff members displayed several possible ways to facilitate this hold (standing side by side, sitting on a chair or floor, etc.) and we selected the position most comfortable for us. Participants were invited to opt out of this exercise and choose what felt most safe for them prior to this exercise.

The entire experience lasted maybe five minutes and there was nothing sexual about it. I was slightly skeptical concerning the benefits of this experiential exercise but afterward understood its significance. The deep wounds from past experiences with men (my father, brother) started to heal as trust was being rebuilt. I would never advise, nor would I practice, physical touch in a counseling setting (Pastoral or Christian counseling setting). However, in the experiential setting in the presence of staff and participants at the Brothers Road JiM weekend, it did seem to serve a therapeutic purpose.

The authors are not recommending Brothers Road, and readers should do their due diligence prior to attending any of their intensives. The use of their MANS principles and Terry's experience at Journey Into Manhood are his alone, based on his personal, lived experience.

Resources for Pornography/ Sex Addiction

As a Therapist, I have walked the journey of recovery with hundreds of men and women as they unravel their life narratives toward healing. Below are treatment resources and protocols that I feel provide the necessary tools for a foundation in recovery for lifelong sexual health. I have used the below programs in clinical practice and in my own recovery.

RECOMMENDED TREATMENT PLANS & RESOURCES

These resources and others can be found on the following website:

Pure Desire Ministries has online programs (Seven Pillars of Freedom & Sex Addiction 101), groups, and counseling for those struggling with sex addiction or betrayal trauma. https://puredesire.org/

The Journey Course by Jay Stringer is another Christian-based program, which is excellent: https://www.thejourneycourse.com/

Betrayal Trauma Resources:

Betrayal and Beyond, by Diane Roberts

https://puredesire.org/

Additional Works of Interest

Gregoire, S. (2021). *The Great Sex Rescue: The Lies You've Been Taught and How to Recover What God Intended*. Baker Books.

Yarhouse, M. (2008). *Sexual Identity and Faith: Helping Clients Find Congruence*. InterVarsity Press.

Yuan, C. (2018). *Holy Sexuality*. Multnomah.

References:

Best ViD. "Beautiful dance Alexandre Desplant 'The Mirror.'" YouTube video, 1:43. September 10, 2016. https://www. youtube.com/watch?v=0iw07Swfxkw.

Brothers Road. (n.d.). Journey into Manhood Weekend Intensive.

Carnes, P. (2001). *Facing the Shadows Workbook: Starting Sexual and Relationship Recovery.* Careerville, MN: Gentle Path Press.

Carnes, P. (2013). *Recovery Starter Kit.* Careerville, MN: Gentle Path Press.

Pure Desire Ministries. (n.d.). Seven Pillars of Freedom. [Curriculum]. Gresham, OR: Pure Desire Ministries.

Pure Desire Ministries. (n.d.). Sex Addiction 101. [Curriculum]. Gresham, OR: Pure Desire Ministries.

Roberts, D. (n.d.). Betrayal & Beyond. Pure Desire Ministries International.

Schnabel, A. O. (2016). Has God Spoken? One Stone.

Senior Officer. (n.d.). Letter in support of PTSD Veteran Administration claim [Letter].

Stringer, J. (n.d.). The Journey Course. Retrieved from https://www.thejourneycourse.com/

Stringer, J. (2018). *Unwanted: How Sexual Brokenness Reveals Our Way to Healing.* InterVarsity Press.

The Lockman Foundation. (1995). *The New American Standard Bible (NASB).* Lockman Foundation.

Weiss, R. (2005). Cruise control: Understanding sex addiction in gay men. Alyson Books.

Yuan, C. (2018). *Holy Sexuality.* Multnomah.

Endnotes

1   1 Corinthians 6:11

2   James McGreevey, Resignation Address (speech, August 12, 2004, New Jersey State House) https://www.americanrhetoric.com/speeches/ jamesmcgreeveyresignation.htm.

3   Matthew 8:53

4   Colossians 1:13

5   Sometimes, even when our conscious minds don't remember things, our physical bodies "remember" past traumatic experiences and their associated emotions.

6   1 Samuel 26:24

7   Romans 15:7

8   Proverbs 23:26

9   Brothers Road teachings contributed substantively to the ideas in this chapter and are used with permission.

10   https://brothersroad.org/surrender/

11   1 Peter 2:11

12   Philippians 4:19

13   Matthew 6:5

14   1 Corinthians 16:13

15   Dobson, J. C (2001). Bringing Up Boys (p. 120). Tyndale House Publishers, Inc. Kindle Edition.